Survey of the Old Testament

Appropriate for All Ages

Teresa Failor

WESTBOW
P R E S S°
A DIVISION OF THOMAS NELSON
& ZONDERVAN

Unless otherwise noted, all scripture is from the King James Version of the Bible.

Scripture quotations taken from the Amplified® Bible (AMP), Copyright © 2015 by The Lockman Foundation. Used by permission. www.Lockman.org

WestBow Press books may be ordered through booksellers or by contacting:

WestBow Press
A Division of Thomas Nelson & Zondervan
1663 Liberty Drive
Bloomington, IN 47403
www.westbowpress.com
1 (866) 928-1240

Because of the dynamic nature of the Internet, any web addresses or links contained in this book may have changed since publication and may no longer be valid. The views expressed in this work are solely those of the author and do not necessarily reflect the views of the publisher, and the publisher hereby disclaims any responsibility for them.

Any people depicted in stock imagery provided by Thinkstock are models, and such images are being used for illustrative purposes only. Certain stock imagery © Thinkstock.

ISBN: 978-1-5127-7556-3 (sc)
ISBN: 978-1-5127-7555-6 (e)

Library of Congress Control Number: 2017902563

Print information available on the last page.

WestBow Press rev. date: 03/13/2017

References:

Holy Bible, Collins World King James Version Study Bible
The Reese Chronological Bible, King James Version 12th edition
Young's Analytical Concordance to the Bible
Smith's Bible Dictionary
The Amplified Bible
Adam Clarke's Commentary on the Holy Bible
The American Heritage College Dictionary

Dates are all approximate as they differ somewhat from source to source.

Teresa C. Failor, February 2017

The Books of the Old Testament in the order they are placed for this study:

Genesis
Exodus
Job
Leviticus
Numbers
Deuteronomy
Joshua
Judges
Ruth
I Samuel
II Samuel
I Chronicles 1-29
I Kings 1-6
II Chronicles1-6
Song of Solomon
II Chronicles 7-10
I Kings 7-11
Proverbs
Ecclesiastes
I Kings 12-22
II Chronicles 11-22
II Kings 1-25
II Chronicles 23-24
Jonah
II Chronicles 25-36
Joel
Amos
Hosea
Isaiah 1-9
Micah
Nahum
Isaiah 10-66
Zephaniah
Habakkuk
Jeremiah 1-52
Ezekiel
Obadiah
Lamentations
Daniel 1- 4, 7-8, 5, Note regarding Persia, 6, 9-12
Psalms (not all of them)
Ezra 1-4
Haggai
Ezra 5-10
Esther
Zechariah
Nehemiah
Malachi

Suggestions for study:

- The scripture references on the left are those suggested for all readers, including the very young. Asterisk lines are provided as a suggestion for one study period.
- In the next column to the right are brief explanations and other helpful information. The scriptures mentioned in those explanations can be studied for those who want to go deeper. When the information states to "see" a certain scripture, it is to be looked up and read by all. Obviously, it is the reader's choice as to whether all the verses will be read, even those not mentioned in the study.
- Additional information is provided from time to time throughout this study. Pertinent notes are added in italics including some of the prophesies related to the coming of the Messiah. Keep in mind one of the main themes of Scripture is to maintain an appropriate lineage for the Messiah. At times, it was necessary for Almighty God to destroy much evil to maintain this lineage. (See the appendix for why we need the Old Testament - *More of God's Purposes for the Written Word.*)
- Definitions that occur in the study are explanations of words in the King James Version, from which this study was prepared, in order to get a more accurate message. Keep in mind the modern translations are easier to read, but this study is an attempt to maintain the original meanings. Difficult words and expressions have been researched to bring clarity to the King James rendering of the Scriptures.
- Follow along with the dates provided to know approximately what time period is indicated.
- **Scriptures that are noted in bold print and underlined are links to New Testament events and fulfillments.** Finding all of the prophesies and matching them with the New Testament scriptures would be a study in itself.
- Mention is made throughout regarding suggested scriptures for memorization.
- Informational pages such as: Exit from Egypt, Maps information, Tribes, Kings, Isaiah 15 & 16 references, More of God's Purposes for Old Testament Scriptures, etc. can be located in the appendix at the end of this study.

Chart of how God set up the required lineage for saving mankind - Adam through Jacob

This is a Bible reading to highlight one of the important purposes of the Scriptures - The lineage of Jesus. Other purposes can be found as one looks more deeply into Scripture.

At a point in time, God needed a young woman who had the appropriate genealogy for Almighty God to place Jesus into her womb. He needed a perfect man (Jesus the Messiah) to become the sacrifice for the salvation of all mankind.

Mary was a human born of two human parents, lived, committed sins, needed a savior, and died just like all of us. The Bible shows that Mary's ancestors were God fearing people and also states that Jesus was her savior.

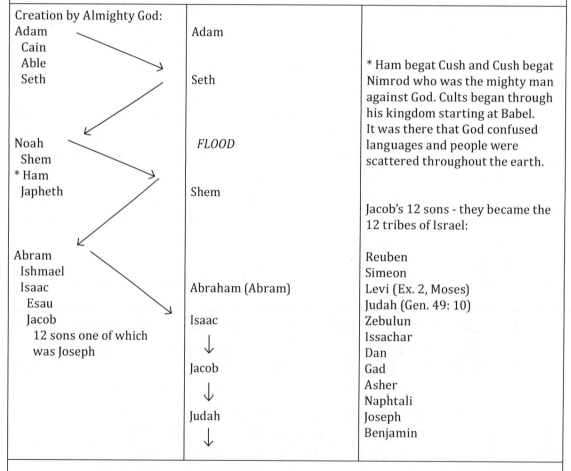

Creation by Almighty God:
Adam
  Cain
  Able
  Seth

Noah
  Shem
* Ham
  Japheth

Abram
  Ishmael
  Isaac
   Esau
   Jacob
    12 sons one of which
    was Joseph

Adam

Seth

FLOOD

Shem

Abraham (Abram)

Isaac
↓
Jacob
↓
Judah
↓

* Ham begat Cush and Cush begat Nimrod who was the mighty man against God. Cults began through his kingdom starting at Babel. It was there that God confused languages and people were scattered throughout the earth.

Jacob's 12 sons - they became the 12 tribes of Israel:

Reuben
Simeon
Levi (Ex. 2, Moses)
Judah (Gen. 49: 10)
Zebulun
Issachar
Dan
Gad
Asher
Naphtali
Joseph
Benjamin

As time went on, many more people populated the earth; therefore, it becomes more difficult to focus on the lineage - but it is there. (See Matthew 1 and Luke 3).

Part 1

(4004 BC)

Genesis

1: 1-31   Creation days 1 - 6 & God's blessing on man . . .

        (You may want to memorize what was created on each of the first 6 days.)

****

2: 1-3,   God rested (meaning stopped working) on day 7 because His work of creation was complete.

  4-17,   Details of creation -

  18-24   Adam named the creatures & Eve was created.

****

3: 1, 6-19,   Disobedience & God's response - **<u>verse 15</u>** is a promise there would be

  20-24   a Messiah.

(4003 BC)

Genesis

4: 1-8,   Cain and Abel were born. God refused Cain's offering & Cain rose up in anger against his brother Abel.

  25-26   Adam and Eve had another son, Seth.

5: 1-3   Chapter 5 lists the generations of Adam.

****

(2448 BC)

Genesis

6: 5-14   The earth was corrupt and God instructed Noah, a descendent of Seth, to build an ark.

7: 1-6   Noah, his family, beasts, and fowls entered the ark. Clean beasts and fowls were for sacrifices; 7 pairs of each of those entered the ark.

(2349 BC)

7: 12,   Noah was 600 years old when they entered the ark; details can be

  17-24   found in verses 7-16.

(2348 BC)

| 8: 13-22 | Noah was 601 when they left the ark (7: 6 he was 600); they were in the ark 1 year and 10 days. Noah built an altar and offered sacrifices. |

****

| 9: 1-4, 6-19 | In verse 6, God commanded man to not destroy human life. Man and woman were to be fruitful and multiply, thus at that time, men were allowed to have more than one wife. The rainbow would be a sign of God's covenant with Noah. |

| 25-29 | Noah's sons were Shem, Ham and Japheth. Verses 20-27 tell of Ham's sin, the curse on him, how it would affect his descendants the Canaanites, and then the blessings on Shem and Japheth. |

(2218 BC)
Genesis

| 10:1, 6-10, 15-20 | The generations of Shem, Ham, and Japheth - Ham was the ancestor of Nimrod who was a mighty hunter before the Lord. That word, before, means against the Lord. The beginning of the kingdom of Babel began there in Shinar. |

(2247 BC)

| 11: 1-9, | This tells about the plan to build the tower of Babel. (The people *is* one means they were in unity and could accomplish anything they imagined.) God scattered the people, their language was confused, and the city was called Babel. |

| 24-32 | In the generations of Shem listed, we can see Abram was a descendent of Noah's son Shem. |

(Ur of the Chaldees - The Chaldees were the people who inhabited the country called Shinar where Babylon was the capital. It was the part of Babylonia that bordered on the Persian Gulf. Other references to the Chaldeans are in II Chronicles 36: 17, Ezra 5: 12, Nehemiah 9: 7, Habakkuk 1: 6, II Kings, Isaiah, Jeremiah, Ezekiel, and Daniel. Keep the beginnings of the Canaanite and Chaldean nations in mind as you continue this study. Haran was in Paddanaram which was also part of the Babylonian Empire at that time - it later fell to the Medes and Persians. The people there were Chaldeans and worshipped the Chaldean gods.)

****

(1921 BC)

Genesis 12: 1-7	God called Abram at age 75. *This calling was a prophesy of future events.* The end of this chapter tells of a famine and Abram went down into Egypt.
13: 1-2, 5-18	Abram and his brother's son, Lot, separated.
14: 18-20	Chapter 14 is the battle of the kings and Abram was victor. More information can be located regarding this king and priest Melchizedek in Hebrews 6:20 to 7: 28.
15: 1-7, 18-21	Chapter 15 is God's promise to Abram that he would have a son and many descendants **(15: 18)**.
16: 1-3, 15-16	Hagar's son was not the son of God's promise to Abram.

(1898 BC)

Genesis 17: 1-8, **19**-22	This tells of God's covenant with Abram and that circumcision would be the sign of the Abrahamic Covenant **(17: 1-13; Galatians 3)**. His name was changed to Abraham; God promised Abraham & Sarah a son, Isaac.

****

18: 1, 17-**18**, 19-21, 33	In chapter 18, God appeared to Abraham and stated that sinful Sodom would be destroyed. Information about the wickedness practiced by the men in Sodom that caused the destruction of Sodom and Gomorrah can be found in 19: 1-7.
19: 4-5, 7, 15-26	Sodom was destroyed. The Lord allowed Lot and his family to be saved; however, his disobedient wife looked back. Chapter 20 tells of Abraham and Sarah's encounter with Abimelech, the king of Gerar.

(1892 BC)

21: 1-5	Isaac was born - verse 12 is a retelling by God that His blessings will come through Abraham's son, Isaac.
22: 1-5,	Abraham was asked to sacrifice Isaac at Mt. Moriah. (Tempt here means to test.) Abraham, by faith, said to the men they were traveling with

11-13,	that he and his son would return. (Genesis15: 6; Romans 4: 3) The Lord provided a sacrifice.
16-19	This is God's response to Abraham's obedience. **(22: 18)**

****

23: 19-20	In chapter 23, Sarah died at age 127 and Abraham purchased a burying place.
24: 3-4, 10, 58-67	Abraham was old. He had his servant promise not to allow Isaac marry a Canaanite woman. Verses 11-57 gives details of finding Rebekah for Isaac.

(1800 BC)
Genesis

25: 1, 7-8,	Abraham married again and died at age 175.
21-34	Twins were born to Isaac and Rebekah (Jacob & Esau). The Lord said the elder shall serve the younger.
26: 3-**4**, 24	God renewed with Isaac the covenant He had with Abraham. Ch. 27 is the details of how Jacob deceived Isaac in order to receive his elder brother, Esau's, blessing. Isaac blessed Jacob instead of Esau.

****

28: 1-5, 12-19,	The blessing of Abraham was passed on to Jacob from his father Isaac. **(28:4)** Jacob obeyed his father's command to find a wife in his relative, Laban's, house. On the journey, he was blessed of the Lord in a dream.
29: 1-6,	Jacob found his wife to be, Rachel. *(Brother in verse 12 means relative. Laban was the brother of Rebekah, Jacob and Esau's mother; Rebekah was the wife of Isaac their father.)* Jacob served Laban 7 years for
10-13, 20	Rachel, but he was given her older sister. Then he served another week, before he was allowed to marry Rachel.

The end of chapter 29 and chapter 30 tell of Jacob's 12 sons being born: Reuben, Simeon, Levi, Judah, Dan, Naphtali, Gad, Asher, Issachar, Zebulun, Joseph and later Benjamin.

****

31: 3, 55	Jacob returned to his homeland. Chapter 31 continues with their journey home.
32: 1-13,	Remember Jacob deceived his father to get the eldest son blessing instead of Esau. On his journey home, he was about to meet Esau.
21, 24-28	Jacob's name was changed to Israel.
33: 1-4,	He met up with his brother Esau; his fear was unfounded.
16-17	Chapter 34 is about Dinah, Leah's daughter.
(1732 BC) Genesis	
35: 1-5,	Jacob built an altar to Almighty God. God changed Jacob's name to Israel and repeated His previous promise.
9-18,	
28-29	Rachel died in childbirth; Benjamin was born. Isaac died at age 180.

****

36: 1, 8	Chapter 36 is about Esau's descendants. Esau dwelt in Mt. Seir. (Esau is Edom - 25:30.)
(1729 BC) Genesis	
37: 3-5, 9-14,	Joseph's dreams - *(Joseph spoke about his dreams to his brothers which caused them to hate him.)*
23-28, Genesis	Of Jacob's 12 sons, he loved Joseph the most; Joseph was sold into Egypt.
37: 31-36	Joseph's brothers told their father that Joseph was dead. Chapter 38 is about Judah's sins.
39: 1-6, 19-23	Potiphar's wife lied about Joseph and he was put into prison.
40: 1-8	This chapter is the prisoners' dreams and Joseph's interpretations as well as the fulfillment. In chapter 40, Joseph is still in prison.

****

(1715 BC)	
41: 1-14,	Pharaoh's dream, the interpretation and Pharaoh's response -
25-48,	Joseph interpreted Pharaoh's dream regarding famine and he was
53-57	assigned to be leader over all Egypt.

****

42: 1-8,	Jacob sent his sons to Egypt for food.
33-34	They were required to bring their youngest brother.
43: 1, 8-9,	Chapters 43 and 44 are about Benjamin taken to Egypt with his
8-9, 16,	brothers.
26-34	

****

(1707 BC)

45: 1-13,	Joseph reveals who he is to his brothers. They were told to bring Jacob
20-28	and dwell safely in Goshen.

(1706 BC)

46: 1-7, 27	Jacob/Israel and all his family, 70 people, go down to Egypt.

****

47: 1-11,	Joseph's family in Egypt - Jacob/Israel was 147 years of age.
27-28	

(1689 BC)

48: 1, 8-14	Israel/Jacob blessed Joseph's sons.
49: 1-2, 8-**10**,	Jacob prophesies over his sons including a prophesy regarding Jesus
33	being from the tribe of Judah. This is mentioned in Matthew 1 and Luke 3. Verse 33 tells of Jacob's death.
50: 12-13,	Jacob's sons did as he had commanded and buried him in the land of
25-26	Canaan. Joseph died at age 110 years.

The end of the book of Genesis

****

(Additional information regarding the exit from Egypt can be found in the appendix.)

(1706 BC)

Exodus

1: 1-17, 22   A new king ruled in Egypt who did not know Joseph. He feared the Israelites would rise up against Egypt because of their great number.

(1571 BC)

Exodus

2: 1-25   Moses was born. Then we read that as an adult, he fled to Midian and married Zipporah the daughter of Reuel (Jethro). The word priest here in the original language could mean either priest or prince. The people of Midian did not worship Almighty God.

(Job would fit here - 1520 BC.
The study of Job is listed after the book of Exodus.)

****

(1491 BC)

3: 1-22   God called Moses.

4: 1-9, 17-23,   This begins with miraculous signs to encourage Moses that the
27-31   Hebrews would believe God had sent him. In verses 10-16, Moses' brother Aaron was to speak for Moses.

5: 1-2, 6-19   Pharaoh would not let the Israelites go out of Egypt and he also increased their oppression. The chapter ends with the people complaining that Moses and Aaron were the cause of their burdens being made heavier.

6: 1-9,   JEHOVAH (He who was, is, and is to come; the Eternal One)...
28-30   The chapter continues with a listing of the tribes of Israel.

(1491 BC)

7: 1-7   Continuing from the previous chapter - God sent the plagues: 7:17
8: 1-2,   waters to blood; 8:5 frogs; 8: 16 lice. (The first three plagues affected
27-32   all the land of Egypt, including Goshen where the Israelites lived.)
9: 1-6, 23-24,   Next: 8: 22-24 was flies; 9: 6 plague on livestock; 9:11 boils; 9: 18 hail;
34-35   10: 14 locusts; and then in10: 22 darkness.

10: 13, 21
11: 1-10 The 10th. plague…

****

12: 1-14, 28, Information on the 10th. plague continues as well as preparation for
32-37, the Passover. Not a bone of the lamb was to be broken; the blood
40-46, from the Passover lamb on the Israelites' doorposts was to cause the
50-51 death angel to pass over those houses. A foreshadowing of Messiah Jesus
can be seen throughout this chapter in the following verses: **7, 13, 23, & 46** (John 19:33). In 15-50 are details regarding the Passover, and their exit from Egypt.

13: 17-22 The first part of chapter 13 is directions for observing Passover when they come into Canaan. Then God gave the reason why He didn't lead them on the shortest way to Canaan (v.17-18).

****

14: 1-2, *(Pihahiroth was a camping place by the Suez Canal between the Red Sea and Mediterranean Sea, Migdol was a camping place on the way to the Red Sea, and Baalzephon was an area southwest of Migdol.)* Pharaoh
5-10, and his army went after the Israelites and they cried out to the Lord.
13-16, The sea opened . . . 600,000 men plus their families and herds walked
19-29, 31 through on dry land. When they went down into Egypt 430 years earlier, there were only 70 men with their families and herds. (Gen. 46: 27; Joseph and his family were already in Egypt.)

(1491 BC)
Exodus
15: 1-2, Verses 1-21 are the songs of Moses and Miriam. Afterwards the people
22-27 murmured because they needed water to drink.
16: 1-4, They murmured again. God sent manna to eat as well as quails. The
12-13, 31 details in chapter 16 are an option for all readers.

17: 1-16 Murmuring for water - Moses struck the rock as God commanded and enough water came out of the rock to supply all those people and their herds! Jehovahnissi - The Lord our banner. (The rock was a type of Christ:

Deuteronomy 32: 3-4, I Corinthians 10: 4, I Peter 2: 7-8, Psalms 18: 2, 31: 3, and Psalms 42, 62, 71, 89, 92, 94.)

(Jethro was also called Reuel and Raguel in Numbers 10:29 and Exodus 2: 15-21 [1571 BC]. Moses fled to Midian and married the daughter of Reuel who lived in Midian. Numbers 10: 29 [1490 BC] tells that Hobab was Reuel's son. Judges 4: 11 [1316 BC] states that Heber the Kenite was a descendant of Reuel's son Hobab. The Kenites were supposedly a branch of the Midianites who remained friendly to the Israelites even when the Midianites were at war with Israel. Also, the meaning of father-in-law in some scriptures could be descendant just as the original word meaning for priest could be priest or prince.)

18: 1-12	Moses' father-in-law came to Moses with Moses' wife and sons.
13-27	After Moses' testimony to Jethro of God's goodness, Jethro rejoiced and offered sacrifices to the Almighty God of Israel.

****

19: 1-6, 17-20 (1491 BC) Exodus	God appeared on Mount Sinai and called Moses up into the mountain.
20: 1-21	The Ten Commandments...

****

(After God used Moses to deliver the Israelites from the evil task masters of Egypt, He gave them laws for living to keep them healthy. He also gave them spiritual laws to teach them right from wrong and how to establish a relationship with Him. They rebelled and disobeyed at times thus many conflicts resulted.)

You may want to memorize the Ten Commandments

****

23: 14-17	In chapters 21 - 23 are laws, ordinances, and feasts - Passover, Pentecost, and Tabernacles.

24: 1-18	The Glory of God ... Moses went up the mountain and was there 40 days and nights.
(1491 BC) Exodus 25: 1-22	This is God's instructions for Moses to build a Sanctuary (a place to meet with God, see verse 8). God would commune with the people through Moses at the Ark of the Covenant - also see Deuteronomy 10: 8. This chapter continues in verses 25-30 with information regarding the Table of Shewbread and in verses 31- 40 the Candlestick.

The actual carrying out of the directions for the tabernacle begins in chapter 35. An in-depth study could be done regarding God's directions for the tabernacle and the carrying out of them, the priest's consecration for their office, the meaning thereof, and how this is foretelling of the Messiah and His people's relationship to Him under the New Covenant.

****

26: 1, 31-34	This is directions for the Tabernacle curtains including the curtain that would separate the Holy Place from the Most Holy Place.

(Later the temple was built from the same pattern. The veil was torn when Jesus died on the cross and the way into the Presence of God was opened to all true believers, Matthew 27:51.

Without the Law these people didn't know what was offensive to God or what pleased Him. They could not grasp the greatness and holiness of Almighty God. This was the reason they were required to set apart Moses' elder brother and his sons as priests unto the Most High God. Even the priests' clothing was to be special. See Exodus 28. It was a symbol of covering their flesh/humanness after the blood sacrifices covered their sins temporarily. The blood sacrifices of animals could not take away their sins; they were dealing with the flesh. See Hebrews 9: 9-15

Aaron, Moses' elder brother, was consecrated as High Priest. He would be allowed to enter the Holy of Holies once each year where God would meet with him regarding the people's sins. If all was not in order when Aaron entered, the bells on the hem of his priestly garment would stop ringing because he would have instantly died!
This is explained in Ex. 28: 35.

The Law was given to show God's people how to live in order to be victorious and fulfilled in their lives as well as be pleasing to God - their loving creator. The Abrahamic Covenant was God's permanent covenant; the Mosaic covenant was to show them their sins until Jesus came. The Law would be in effect until Jesus offered Himself as our sacrifice for sins. At that time, the New Covenant (II Corinthians 5: 21) became effective. That made God's promises to Abraham available to all people, not just the Jews. We now are to look for the principles of the laws, and apply the spiritual significances not the letter of the law. God's moral laws don't change.

Many times instead of the Jews being an example they followed the ungodly practices of the other nations. One of the main themes of this study is to get God's people ready for the Messiah to be born and an opportunity for all people to be saved under the New Covenant.

The beginning chapters of the book of Romans explain life without the law, the reason the law was given, and justification under the New Covenant. These New Testament scriptures are Romans 4: 15 and 7: 7-25.)

(1491 BC)

Exodus

27: 1, 20-21	The furnishing of the tabernacle, altar, offerings, priests, their garments, and holy anointing oil are discussed in Chapter 27. This continues through chapter 31: 18.
28: 1-2, 30-36	Aaron and his sons were set apart; then we can read the directions for making their garments and Aaron's breastplate. Aaron was to follow God's directions exactly and be prepared before entering the Holy of Holies where God would meet with him. If he did not follow God's commands, he would instantly die.
29: 1-2, 43-46	Consecration of the priests and offerings is detailed in this chapter.
30: 1, 10, 25-30	This tells of the altar of incense and holy anointing oil. Before the veil (verse 6) means outside of the Most Holy Place where the Ark of the Covenant would be.

31: 1-12, 18   The Lord gave certain individuals the knowledge and ability to do all that was commanded. He does not require anyone to do something for Him without supplying the ability. God gave Moses commandments on two tablets of stone.

****

Exodus

32: 1-8, 15,   Rebellion! Moses was in the mount 40 days and nights (24: 18).
   19-23,

   30-34   Moses talked to the Lord and God told Moses He would send an angel with him to lead the rebellious people.

33:1-3,

   9-23   Moses prayed and requested that if Your Presence doesn't go, then don't send us. The chapter ends with Moses seeing God's Glory.

****

34: 1-14   This is replacement of the broken tablets. The Lord is speaking with Moses about His covenant with the Israelites. Verses 18-23 are feasts that are to be celebrated annually (Passover, Pentecost, and Tabernacles). When Moses came down from the mount, his face shone with the Glory of God.

Chapters 35-39 are the Word of the Lord concerning the Sabbath, offerings, furniture of the tabernacle including the altar of burnt offerings, and cloths for service.

35: 1,   Moses spoke God's directions to the people. Offerings information and
   30-35   God's anointing for service complete this chapter.

36: 1-7,   The work on the Tabernacle begins in verse 8 and continues to chapter 39:43. In those verses, we can read about offerings and the work being completed.

37: 29

38: 21-26   This tells us the number of Israelite men 20 or more years old was 603,550. Do you remember how many went down into Egypt? (Genesis 46: 26)

39: 1, 30-43   The work was completed and met with Moses' approval; it was as the Lord commanded. (Mitre means the headdress worn by ancient Jewish high priests as in Lev. 8:9)

(1491 BC)
40: 1-2, 17,   This is specific directions regarding the setting up of the tabernacle,
    30-38   then the actual raising, and finally the Glory of God.

The end of the book of Exodus
****

****

(1520 BC)   (*The book of Job would fit after chapter 6 of Exodus.*)
Job
1: 1-5, 20-22   Satan's part in Job's upcoming trials and the listing of them are in this chapter as well as chapter 2.
2: 9, 11   This is Job's wife and friends' response to his situation.
3: 25   The chapter begins with Job's complaint. That which he greatly feared came upon him. He was expecting evil consequences for his children's behavior.

4: 1, 7-8   Eliphaz, Job's friend, tells him that he had received what he deserved for doing some kind of evil. His discourse continues throughout this chapter.

5: 1, 17-20   Eliphaz gives his advice to pray to someone; next is God's correction. In chapters 6 and 7, Job speaks of his anguish and wishes for death.

****

8: 1-6, 20   Another friend, Bildad, speaks.

9: 1, 20   Job acknowledges the difficulty of being guiltless with God. This chapter speaks of Almighty God's greatness.
10: 1-2, 15   Job wants to know what he did wrong.
11: 1-6   Another friend, Zophar, spoke his thoughts which were accusations against Job.

12: 3-4	Job's answer and his confidence in God continues through chapters 13
13: 15-16	and 14.

****

Job

15: 1, 6	Eliphaz speaks again.
16: 1	Job's response to his friends - miserable comforters . . .

17: 10	
18: 5	Bildad speaks again in condemnation throughout chapter 18.
19: 1-2	Job's response. . . In Chapter 20, Zophar spoke again about the
21: 34	judgment of the wicked. Job's response is in chapter 21.
22: 1-5	Eliphaz spoke exhorting him to repent.
23, 25-27	
23: 1-3	Job declared his confidence in God but he couldn't find Him. This continues in chapter 24. In chapter 25, Bildad reproved Job and his answer is in chapters 26 - 31. Job protests against their condemnation and declares himself innocent.

32: 1- 5, 12, 21-22	Elihu was the youngest, thus he waited till all had spoken. He said he would not be influenced by any man's speaking. He continues through chapter 37 and declares the greatness of God's works, and that He is just. God calls man to repentance; He can not be unjust.

Job

33: 1-5	
34: 12	
36: 1-7, 26-33	

****

37: 1-14 23-24	The greatness of God proclaimed . . .
38: 1-7	The Lord answered Job's complaints by asking where was Job when God created everything and provided all our blessings with His great power. The Lord's answer continued in chapter 39 through 40: 1.

40: 2-5	Job responded and the Lord answered again. (The Lord's answers in these chapters can be read to remind us of the greatness of God's power and love.) Chapter 41 tells of the great power of God and continues throughout the chapter.
42: 1- 17	Job answers the Lord. The Lord's anger was kindled against Job's friends. He instructed Job to offer burnt sacrifices to Him on behalf of Job's friends, and pray for them. Job's blessings are recorded, which were greater than he had before his trials.

The end of the book of Job

****

(The New Testament teaches that when we believe God's promises in our hearts [the written Word], speak it with our mouths, and believe we have received, we shall have what we say. Following are scriptures that can be studied to provide information regarding out new and better Covenant:

Fear - Genesis 15: 1; Isaiah 41: 10, 13; Proverbs 29: 25 & 10: 24; I John 4: 18; II Timothy 1: 7.

Faith - Hebrews 11: 1 & 6; Matthew 9: 22, 29, 17: 20 & 21: 22; Mark 5: 34 & 11: 23- 24; Romans 3: 28, 4: 5, 10: 17, 12: 3, & 14: 23; James 1: 6.

Two Covenants - Galatians 4: 21-31; Hebrews 7: 19, 22; & 8:6. To partake of this New Covenant, we must believe in our heart that Jesus paid for our sins by shedding His blood on the cross, and He was raised from the dead, then submit to Him and confess with our mouth that He is our Lord, Romans 10: 9-10.)

****

The book of Leviticus is God giving laws and regulations for the people under the Old Covenant and instructions to the priests who were responsible for carrying out the instructions. It also states the blessings for obedience and curses for rebellion/ disobedience. The theme is the holiness of God and His spiritual/moral laws do not change with the New Covenant.

Leviticus chapter topics; to be read as desired:

1-7	Laws about offerings and sacrifices
8-10	Ordination of Aaron and his sons as priests
11-15	Laws about ritual cleanness and uncleanness
16	The Day of Atonement (Keep in mind what Jesus went through to pay for our sins. His atonement was a one time event instead of annual.)
17-27	Laws about holiness in life and worship.

(1490-1451 BC)
Leviticus
16: 1-34

****

17: **11**-14   The blood of slain beasts -
Only Aaron, the anointed High Priest, could go within the veil into the Holy of Holies. He was required to offer a sin offering before he entered. Only the blood sacrifice makes an atonement for the sinner. Chapter 18 is commandments regarding unlawful marriage and lusts.

19: 18   A repetition of numerous laws follow. Love thy neighbor as thyself. The laws continue to the end of this book.

23: 3-16, 34   This tells of the feasts of the Lord: the Sabbath day of rest, Passover, Unleavened Bread, Firstfruits (fulfilled with Jesus' death, burial, and resurrection), and Pentecost (fulfilled in Acts 2: 1-4 with the coming of the Holy Spirit). The chapter continues with more feasts and

39-43   ends with directions for the Feast of Tabernacles that is yet to be fulfilled. In the following chapters are more laws for living, including

27: 34   blessings and curses.

The end of the book of Leviticus
****

****

(1490 - 1451 BC)

Numbers

1: 1-4	The numbering of the tribes is in chapters 1 & 2.
2: 17	This tells where they will pitch their tents in relation to the Tabernacle. (See chart in the appendix.)
3: 6-7	The priests (Aaron and his sons), and the Levites, men from the tribe of Levi, were to do the service of the Tabernacle. A chart in the appendix shows where they camped. Chapter 4 describes the duties of the priest's office and then the Levites were numbered. In Chapter 5, there are more laws and in chapters 6-7 we can see blessings and offerings information. Chapter 8 is also about the Levites.
9: 1-2, 11-18,	The instructions for observing the Passover is repeated, then verses 19-23 continue regarding the cloud from God.

Numbers

10: 11-13, 33-36	They began their journey out of the wilderness of Sinai.
11: 4, 10-17 31-35	The people murmured for meat to eat and Moses complained to the Lord as to the great burden of over 600,000 people (Ex. 12:37). God gave help to Moses, then He sent them quail; however, they were punished for their murmuring.

****

12: 1-9	In chapter 12, Miriam and Aaron, Moses' sister and brother, spoke against him; God punished them.
13: 1-3, 17-18, 25-33	Moses sent a man from every tribe to spy out the land of Canaan that the Lord promised to them. Caleb said they were well able to be victorious over the Canaanites but the people still resisted.
14: 2-3, 9-11, 17-24, 27-34,	This tells of the spies doubt and unbelief, then Joshua and Caleb's declaration. The Lord was provoked, and Moses prayed. The Lord declared that they would wander in the wilderness 40 years due to their unbelief in Him and His promises. The adults who murmured would all die in the wilderness; their children, who would

| 42-45 | then be grown, will possess the Promised Land. They rebelled again and brought evil upon themselves. |

****

Chapter 15 states laws for when they would come into their new land. Murmuring against Moses and Aaron continue in chapter 16 as well as rebellion that provoked God's anger. In 17-19 there are more laws and ordinances for the people of Israel.

Numbers

| 20: 1-2, 7-12 | Miriam died. Their journey continued. The people complained again because there was no water. Their complaints provoked Moses to disobedience. Because of this, Moses and Aaron were denied entrance into the promised land. See the following note. |

(The rock, being a type of Christ, was to be struck only one time. Information regarding this can be found in the note at Exodus 17: 6-7 where Moses struck the rock the first time. Jesus would die only one time to pay for the sins of all mankind forever. The Old Testament is not only a means of learning for us but the prophesies and events are a foreshadowing of the coming Messiah and end times. The command of the Lord was to speak to the rock this time and Moses struck it. It was necessary for a discipline to be applied due to the magnitude of what the rock represented. Because of that, Moses was denied entrance into the Promised Land. He would not be the leader to take the people in. For more information on the preceding, see the note in the Amplified Bible at Numbers 20.)

| 21: 1-10 | Verse 10 and forward is their continued journey- see appendix. |
| 22: 1-6, 18 | Balak, king of Moab, was attempting to get the prophet Balaam to curse the Israelites and the angel of the Lord opposed Balaam (v. 22- 35). *(God had already spoken to Balaam but he continued to ask again- three times in all. Balaam worshiped Almighty God but also knew the forbidden art of divination.)* |

23: 8, 18-20

| 24: 2-16, **17-18**, 25 | Throughout chapter 24 is murmuring as well as more about the prophet Balaam and King Balak. Israel provoked God's anger again by worshiping the gods of Moab in chapter 25. |

****

26: 4, 65	Chapters 26-30 are laws: numbering of the people, feasts, offerings, and other laws.
31: 1-6, 48-54	Chapter 31 tells of war with Midian, and division of the spoils. *(The reason for the wars was to drive out the ungodly inhabitants of the lands God promised to His people. They were the cause of Israel committing abominations against the Lord - verse 16.)*

(1452 BC)
Numbers

32: 1-5, 16-25, 29-32	The Israelites were now positioned on the East side of the Jordan River. Representatives of the tribes of Reuben and Gad requested they be given that land for their possession. *Regarding their continued journeying and assigning of the tribes inheritances (Numbers 33 & 34), see Bible maps provided for that purpose.*
35: 1-4	The Levites and more laws . . .
36: 1-3, 7-9, 13	This is directions for women who inherited land of their fathers (See also 27: 1-7). This only happened if a man had no son/sons.

The end of the book of Numbers
****

Deuteronomy is the retelling of what has already been written. There is retelling of laws, ordinances, feast days, and all that Moses had previously spoken to the people.

(1451 BC)
Deuteronomy

1: 1-46	Moses is retelling the command to possess the land, and exhortations for obedience.

****

2: 1-3, 25	Chapters 2 and 3 tell of the struggles encountered on the Israelites way to Canaan.
3: 1-2, 21-28	Moses in remembering his disobedience and gave an exhortation for the people to obey.

4: 1-2, 39-40	Do not add to or diminish the Word of God. This command is repeated in the last book of the Bible, Revelation 22: 18-19. The encouragement for obedience continues.
5: 1-21, 27, 30-33	Chapter 5 is a retelling of the Ten Commandments and the Law.

(Review the Ten Commandments.)

****

6: 1-7, 12	Moses spoke the Words of God to the people.
7: 6-9, 12-15	The Hebrews are a special people unto the Lord. Chapter 8 is an exhortation to remember all the miraculous ways the Lord took care of
8: 6-20	them 40 years in the wilderness. Obey God; it is He who gives His people the power to prosper, not ourselves. Even though the Israelites were disobedient and sometimes rebellious, God still took care of them.
9: 1-6	Go in and possess the land. The chapter continues with reminding the people of their rebellion in the wilderness. This theme continues in chapter 10.
10: 1-5, 12-13, 17-18	The two tablets were restored. God takes special care of the fatherless and widows. The retelling continues regarding worship and offerings.

****

11: 1-2, 7-8, 13-25	
12: 23-24, 32	This chapter is about offerings and food. Chapter 13 tells of false prophets; chapter 14 is more about food and offerings.
15: 7-8	In chapter 16 feasts are listed: Passover, Pentecost, and Tabernacles. Laws and ordinances continue in the following chapters.
17: 18-20	Duties of a king . . .
18: 9, 22,	False prophets . . .
15, 18-19	This is a prophesy of the coming Messiah.

****

Deuteronomy

20: 1-4	Regarding battles and sieges . . . Chapter 21 covers laws concerning rebellion and murder.
22: 5	Laws continue throughout the following chapters (23: 24-25; 24: 19-22; 26: 16-19; 27: 9-10) with curses for disobedience in chapter 27. See Matthew 22: 37- 40 to discover how this all applies to the New Covenant. Jesus gave us two new commandments that He said covers all the law and the prophets. God's moral laws never change.
28: 1-13	Chapter 28: 1-13 is blessings then the curses for disobedience. See Galatians 3: 13-14, 29.
30: 5-10, 19-20	Chapters 29 and 30 continue the exhortation to obedience and its blessings.

****

31: 6-8	God's charge to Joshua is in chapter 31. God is speaking in **32: 21**
32: 1-4, 44-52	about a nation that will move Israel to jealousy at a future time - meaning the Gentiles in the New Covenant. Next is Moses' song and the end of his life.
33: 1	Moses blessed the children of Israel in chapter 33.
34: 1-12	Moses died being a healthy man at age 120 according to verse 7; Joshua had been commissioned to lead the people into the Promised Land. (See Num. 20: 8-12, Deut. 32: 4, and the note after Num. 20.)

(We are now under a New Covenant. Jesus paid the price for our sins and in the New Testament promises that if we are Christ's, then we are Abraham's seed, and heirs according to the promises made to Abraham as recorded in Galatians 3.)

You may want to memorize the books of the Bible thus far.

The end of the book of Deuteronomy
****

****

(1451 BC)

Joshua	Joshua, the successor of Moses, led the Israelites, east to west, across the Jordan River which is north of the Dead Sea. After they crossed, they were facing Jericho (see map). This book also tells of the fall of Jericho, the battle at Ai, and renewal of God's covenant with His people.
1: 1-9	The Lord is speaking to Joshua . . .
10-16	This is Joshua speaking to the people and their answer. (Verse 12 is about the tribes that Moses gave an inheritance on the east side of the Jordan. See Numbers 32: 5.)
2: 1-4, 9-14, 24	Rahab hid the spies; she provided protection for them.
3: 1-3, 10-17	They were now on their way to Jericho.

****

4: 13-14, 19	The number of the new generation of men was 40,000.
5: 1, 4-7, 10-12	When Passover was celebrated the manna ceased.
6: 1-20, 24-25	This is instructions for taking the city of Jericho.

****

Joshua 7: 2-11, 19	In chapter 7, Achan had stolen silver, gold, and garments from the spoils in the city of Jericho and hid them. Because of his sin, the Lord was not with them when Israel fled before the people of Ai. His sin was found out, and he was punished. Then . . .
8: 1, 18, 30-35	The city of Ai was taken causing the nations around them to be afraid.
9: 1-9, 11, 14-16, 22-25	The Gibeonites. . . Not seeking God's wisdom regarding the Gibeonites caused Israel much trouble.

****

(1451 BC)
Joshua
10: 1-8,   Chapter 10 tells of Israel's battles; the Lord gave them victory.
    12-14,   The chapter continues with the sun and moon miracle and more
    40-43   victories.

(1450 BC)   (Houghed/*hocked* meaning the joint, near the foot, bending backwards
11: 5-8,   in the back legs of the horses was disabled.) The battles and victories of
    18-20   Israel continued, and chapter 12 is a listing of conquered kings.

(1445 BC)   Chapters 13 through 21 are the dividing of the land and assigning
13: 1, 7   the tribes inheritances. These can be viewed on a Bible History map.
(1444 BC)
14: 10-11   Caleb was strong at age 85. (Joshua and Caleb were the only two Israelite
             men entering Canaan who came out of Egypt with Moses.)
21: 43-45   The Lord's Word came to pass.

22: 1-6   After all the victories, the two tribes and the half tribe who had taken
             their inheritance on the East side of Jordan were ready to go home.
             Joshua charged them to continue to obey the Lord and he blessed them.
             There was a dispute regarding an altar in 10-34 but it was resolved.

****

23: 1-8, 14 Joshua's last words to the Israelites are in chapters 23 - 24.
             Chapter 24 is Joshua's exhortation regarding God's victories for them,
             and their fathers, when they came out of Egypt. Joshua died at age 110.
(1427 BC)
Joshua
24: 1-17,   Joseph had died in Egypt and his bones, which were brought up out of
    20-24,   Egypt, were buried in Shechem. Then Aaron's son, Eleazar, died.
    29, 32   (See the end of Joshua 24: 15 in KJV:
             ". . . As for me and my house, we will serve the Lord".)

The end of the book of Joshua
****

****

(1425 BC)

Judges

1: 1-4, 16, 21, 27, 31, 33	Joshua died; who will lead? More battles - The tribes did not drive out all the inhabitants of Canaan.
2: 1-23	This is retelling of Joshua's death and the Israelites falling into the idol worship practiced by the people around them. The Israelites did evil; God in His mercy gave them judges, but they still disobeyed.
3: 1-11,	The Lord did not drive out some of the nations in order to test Israel's obedience to Him. The children of Israel did evil again then cried out to the Lord for help. God gave them a judge; they had peace for 40 years. Beginning in verse 12, they continued to do evil and served
30-31	Eglon, King of Moab, 18 years. When they finally called out to God, the Lord, in His great mercy, gave them Judge Ehud.
4: 1-9, 23-24	In chapter 4, we can see that Judge Deborah was also a Prophetess of God. He caused her to triumph in battle against the king of Canaan.

****

5: 1-3, 31	Deborah's song of praise to the Lord continues throughout chapter 5. The Lord raised up Gideon/Jerubbaal in chapter 6.
6: 1-16, 33-40	Gideon destroyed Baal's altar and led the Israelites against the Midianites. Chapter 6 ends with the sign Gideon received from the Lord. After Gideon, there were more judges.

****

Judges

7: 1-7, 23	Gideon obeyed God and prevailed against the Midianites with only 300 men.
8: 22-23, 28, 32-35	The battle with Midian continues through chapter 8 and Midian was subdued. After Gideon's death, the children of Israel rebelled against God again.
9: 1-4, 7,	Abimelech, one of Gideon's sons, slew his brothers in order to become the next king (Light here means unstable; vein means outgoing.); however, his youngest brother Jotham escaped. This chapter continues

55-57	in verse 7 with a parable by Jotham against Abimelech and Abimelech's battles.
10: 5-18	The judge in Israel after Abimelech was Tola then Jair became judge.
11: 4-6, 32	The Ammonites oppressed Israel; the Ephraimites were conquered in Chapter 12.

****

(1161 BC)
Judges

13: 1-25	There was a call of God on Samson's life before he was born. Sampson was born.
16: 28-30	Chapters 14 - 16 are exploits of Sampson and the end of 16 records his death.
17: 5-11	This tells of Micah's idolatry.
18: 1-2, 14-15, 18-20	Without a Godly judge or king to lead them, the Israelites, even the Levites, quickly fell into grievous sin. Chapter 19 records the wickedness of the Gibeonites.
20: 11-13, 26-28, 46-47	Israel coming against the tribe of Benjamin (That's where the Gibeonites dwelt - 19: 14.) continues in verses 14-48.
21: 2-3, 13, 17, 24-25	In chapter 21, we can read of more wickedness and struggles, then a plan for restoration of the tribe of Benjamin. There was no one to keep them following the Lord. They needed a king.

****

The end of the book of Judges
****

(1322 - 1312 BC)
Ruth

1: 1-8, 15, 22	Ruth wouldn't leave her mother-in-law, and she chose to serve Naomi's God.

2: 1-23   *(The Israelites were commanded by their law to be merciful to the poor by not reaping the corners of their fields. See Leviticus 19: 9. If a sheaf should be accidentally left in the field, it was to remain there for the poor. Ruth also had God's favor.)*

In chapter 3, Ruth gained favor with Boaz.

4: 9-17   Eventually she was blessed with a good husband and their son was the grandfather of King David meaning they were in the lineage of Jesus. *(The early lineage was covered at the beginning of this study.)*

Review book memorization and add the next three: Joshua, Judges, Ruth.

The end of the book of Ruth
****

(1171 BC)
I Samuel

1: 1, 9-11, 20, 27-28   Hannah prayed for a man child. He was born and she promised God he would be a servant of the Lord.

2: 1-4, 8, 11, 18-21   Hannah's rejoicing continues. Horn means strength. Samuel became a prophet of God. Chapter 2 continues with information about the wicked sons of Eli the priest.

(1165 BC)
I Samuel
3: 1-14, 19-20   The Lord spoke to Samuel regarding punishment of Eli's sons for their evil ways. Samuel was established as a prophet.

****

4: 1, 10-11, 15	The Ark of God was in the possession of the Philistines. Eli's sons were slain. Eli died as well as his daughter-in-law. Details of Ichabod's birth are recorded in verses 19-22.
5: 1-8	The Ark of God was taken to Ashdod, a city West of Jerusalem close to the Mediterranean Sea. Then it was sent to Gath which is southeast of Ashdod. Cities and places mentioned throughout can be located on a Bible study map. (milch kine - cow)
6: 1-3, 7-8, 12-15, 20-21	The Philistines returned the Ark to Bethshemesh.
7: 1-10, 13-17	The Ark was then taken to Kirjathjearim.

****

8: 1-7, 19-22	Israel wanted a king. The Lord instructed Samuel to give them a king. Samuel told all the words of the Lord regarding how a king would make himself rich and demand the people to be his servants. They still wanted a king (verses 11- 8).
(1095 BC) I Samuel 9: 1-2, 15-17, 27	Saul came to Samuel; this continues in chapter 10.
10: 1, 5-6, 9, 24-26	Saul was anointed and chosen to be their king. The chapter can be read completely to obtain more details.
11: 1, 5-6, 8, 11, 15	The Ammonites camped against (besieged) Jabesh. They asked to make a covenant with them and they would serve. Samuel reminded the people of how the Lord took care of them and their fathers, but they stopped trusting the Lord. The asking for a king continued then Samuel comforts the people.
12: 1-2, 12-25	

****

13: 1-2, 9-14	More battles with the Philistines. . . Saul disobeyed . . . The battle with the Philistines continued.

14: 1, 6,   Jonathan, Saul's son . . .
   20-23

   46, 52   Conflicts with the Philistines continued all the days of Saul.

15: 1, 7-31,   Wars continued and Saul blamed the people for his sin instead of repenting before God.

   35   The Lord rejected Saul from being king. (See Proverbs 16:18-19)

****

16: 1-13   David was anointed to be king.

(1063 BC)

I Samuel

17: 4-11,   Goliath defies the armies of Israel.

   16-18,   Jesse sent David to where his brothers were engaged in a battle.

  32, 40-45, David will go to fight Goliath.

   49-50,   (staff meaning a rod) David killed Goliath because he had defied the

  55-56, 58 Lord's army. King Saul called for David.

****

18: 1-2, 12,   In chapter 18, David and Saul's son Jonathan became friends. King Saul

   28-30   was jealous of David because of his victory over Goliath.

            In 19 & 20 he is seeking to kill David, and chapter 21 tells of David's activities as he flees from Saul.

22: 1-2,   Saul had the priests of the Lord killed because they knew where David

   9-10,   was and did not tell Saul.

   17-18

23: 1-4,   Keilah was the city where descendants of Calob (one of the 2 men of the

   26-29   original generation coming out of Egypt who were allowed to enter the promised land) settled. There were more pursuits of David by King Saul, then the Philistines invaded the land.

24: 1-2,   Verses 3-22 give an account of how David overcame Saul and Saul's

   16-18   response.

25: 1-3,   This chapter begins with Prophet Samuel's death. Nabal refused
  9-11,   to help David; however, Abigail provided the food David needed for
  35-38   himself and his men. David was pacified. There are more details of these
            encounters in this chapter.

****

26: 1-2, 6-18, Saul continues to pursue David in chapter 26.

(Even though David knew he was to be the next king, he would not harm King Saul because he had been anointed of God to be Israel's first king. That's why David addressed him as the Lord's anointed. David trusted the Lord to keep him safe as Saul pursued him.)

27: 1-7   In order to be safe from Saul, David dwelt with the Philistines for a period of time.

28: 4-7   The Philistines prepared to fight against Israel. Samuel was dead and the Lord had departed from Saul; he was unable to hear from the Lord. Saul sinned again. Attempting to obtain advice, he contacted a woman who had a familiar (evil) spirit. Chapter 28 gives the details of this encounter. The Lord had removed the kingdom from Saul and gave it to David.

(1056 BC)
30: 26   Chapters 29 and 30 are more battles and David's victories; the
31: 6   Philistines fought against Saul (Israel) in chapter 31 and he died.

The end of the book of I Samuel
****

****

(1056-1017 BC)
II Samuel   David was told that Saul and Jonathan had died. Saul's son Jonathan
1: 1-4   was David's friend. The rest of the chapter is David's lament over their deaths.

2: 1-11, 17-18	David, directed by God, went to Hebron and was anointed king of Judah. Ishbosheth, Saul's son, was king over Israel and David was king over Judah. (Abner was a servant of Ishbosheth, and Joab, son of Jeruiah, was a servant of David.)
3: 1-2, 17-21, 25-28, 30, 37-39	This continues with a list of David's sons, then Abner went to David to make peace between Israel and Judah. Joab didn't believe Abner . . .

****

4: 5-6, 10-12	Rechab and Baanah, two Israelites, killed the king of Israel (Saul's son) believing David would reward them.

(1048 BC)

II Samuel

5: 1-5, 10, 17-25	David was anointed king over Israel. The Philistines came against King David.
6: 1-19, 23	The Ark of God was carried from the house of Abinadab into the house of Obededom. Then the Ark was taken to the City of David. (Perezuzzah: Perez was of the tribe of Judah and uzzah meant broken)

****

7: 1-29	The Lord was speaking to the Prophet Nathan regarding David and his kingdom; David would always have a descendant on the throne. **(7: 12-16).** David's prayer. . .
8: 15-18	David's victories . . . David reigned over all Israel.

(1040 BC)

9: 1, 6-7, 13	Chapter 9 shows David's kindness to Mephibosheth, Saul's descendant. Saul's son, Jonathan, had been David's friend. Chapter 10 describes more battles and David's victories. Chapter 11 is about David's sin, and family issues are discussed in chapters 12 - 14. (Chapter 14 is dated 1027 BC.)

****

(1024 BC)

15: 1-6,	Chapters 15-22 record conspiracy against David by Absalom his son,
12-13	then more battles.

18: 1-5, 15,	King David performed his duty even though he was concerned about
	his son. Verses 6 - 31 describe Absalom's death and two men reporting
31-33	their victory in battle to the king.

(1023 BC)

19: 1-2, 22	King David continued to grieve over Absalom.

(1022 BC)

20: 1-2	More revolt . . .

(1021 BC)

II Samuel

21: 1-6,	The Lord sent a famine because Israel broke their promise to the
20-22	Gibeonites (Joshua 9: 14-15). They were avenged, see verse 9, then there
	were 4 more battles with the Philistines. The Lord delivered David from
	his enemies.

****

II Samuel

(1018 BC)

22: 1-7,	Chapter 22 is David's song of thanksgiving; it is good for all to read
29-34,	in its entirety.
47-51	

****

23: 1-5	This chapter continues with David's discourse regarding his men.
24: 1-4,	David was incited by Satan to number the people. (See I Chron. 21: 1.)
9-25	

The end of the book of II Samuel

****

The end of Part I

****

Part 2

As the earth became more and more populated, the issues grew larger and more numerous. The Jews even fought among themselves. At one point, after the death of King Solomon, Israel split; 2 tribes were Judah, and the other 10 were Israel.

God's people rebelling and worshipping idols caused their Babylonian exile; His purpose was to bring the Israelites back to Himself - restored as a God fearing nation. Throughout Samuel to Malachi, we can read about the carrying away of God's people to Babylon, and the return to their homeland. First there are prophesies of this exile and prophesies of their return. After the prophesies, was the actual time of being besieged and exiled. (For prophesies of their return from exile see Jeremiah 29 & 30, Ezra 1, and Isaiah 44 & 45.)

Years before Cyrus was born, God's prophet foretold that King Cyrus of Persia would be the one allowing the Jews to return to their homeland and rebuild. That prophesy included his name. The actual working out of their return was over a period of years. Their release, the rebuilding of the temple and other houses, as well as rebuilding the walls of Jerusalem are documented. We learn also that all the Jews did not return; some chose to stay in Babylon and the surrounding areas. Those who returned did so under one nation called Israel. They were no longer split; the city of Jerusalem, where the temple was rebuilt, was their center of worship. A Kings and Prophets chart is in the appendix.

Keep in mind, as you continue this study of the Old Testament, that the men of God who approved the original Scriptures as God's Word did not put the Bible together in date order. Therefore, this Part 2 study has revised the usual order of books in the current Bibles to better fit the chronology of events. Even the chapters in some of the books are not necessarily in chronological order such as Daniel, Isaiah, Ezekiel, and others. If a more precise dating arrangement is desired, see a Chronological Bible. Another factor is that all available study books do not have identical dating. However, they should be accurate enough for a realistic Bible study.

The prophets Jeremiah, Daniel, Ezekiel, Haggai, Zechariah, and Malachi all prophesied during at least part of the time of the Babylonian captivity and return. Ezra the priest and scribe as well as Nehemiah were from that time period also. That should help to explain why the books and chapters are intermingled at times in their chronological order. This study has arranged the dating semi-chronological so that the order of events may not confuse anyone.

I Kings thru Malachi
(The dating for Chronicles is before Kings)

(I Chronicles covers the time period from the book of Genesis through II Samuel and I Kings chapter 2. The genealogies are transcribed in chapters 1 - 9 as found in a book that was carried to Babylon in the time of the captivity. It is believed that Ezra the Priest and Scribe compiled that book.)

****

(1520 BC)
Job is covered in Part 1.
****

(I Chronicles chapters are dated as follows:
- *Chapter 2 (1471 BC),*
- *Ch. 3 (1053 BC),*
- *Ch. 4 & 5 (1300 BC),*
- *Ch. 6 (1280 BC),*
- *Ch. 7 & 8 (1400 BC),*
- *Ch. 9 (1200 BC),*
- *Ch. 10 (1056 BC),*
- *Ch. 13 (1058 BC), etc.*

Thus we can see that Holy Scriptures were compiled from the original documents for reasons other than chronology. As you go through this study, keep in mind the dates may not all be exact.)

****

I Chronicles

(1200 BC)	Chapter 1 is the genealogy from Adam to Abraham. This
I Chronicles	continues through chapters 2 - 9.
9: 1-2	Genealogies continue with Priests, Levites, and Nethinims (temple slaves - those who remained of the Gibeonites). See Josh 9:21.

(1056 BC)
I Chronicles
10: 1-3, 13   Saul died in battle with the Philistines.

(1047 BC)
11: 1-7   David became king, fought against the Jebusites, and dwelt in the City of David. More battles and listing of those who fought with David appear in chapter 12.

12: 1-2   Chapter 12 lists David's warriors - then in chapter 13, David had the Ark of the Covenant placed in the home of Obededom for 3 months. In Chapter 15 it was taken to the City of David where he had prepared a place for the Ark of God.

14: 8-10,   The Philistines came against David.
   16-17   God was with him.

15: 11-12   See Exodus 25: 8-22. (Exodus 28 & 29 tell of the consecration required of priests to minister in the priests office.)
   14-16, 28

****

(1042 BC)
16: 1, 4,   This is rejoicing, singing, offerings to God, appointing of Levites
   7-36   to minister, then praises to God.

17: 3-15,   **(17: 12-14)**
   20-22

****

      Chapters 18 to 20 are David at war with the Philistines, Syrians, and
21: 1-2, 7-8   Ammonites. David numbered Israel in Chapter 21.

(1017 BC)
I Chronicles
22: 6-10   David charged Solomon to build the House of the Lord.
23: 1   Solomon was appointed by God to be king after David. Chapter 23: 2 through Chapter 27 is the numbering of the Levites for service, divisions, and offices.

28: 2-6, 20	God proclaimed that Solomon would build the House of the Lord. Next we see David speaking to the Princes of Israel.
29: 13-29	Offerings . . . David died.

I Chron. 29: 14 KJV - "All things come of Thee, and of thine own have we given thee."

The end of the book of I Chronicles

****

Note: David's reign - He reigned 40 years over Israel and died at age 70. (II Sam. 5: 4, I Kings 2:11). The only kings of Israel who lived more than 60 years were David, Solomon, and Manasseh. (Solomon's reign - I Kings 2: 12) It was during Solomon's reign the first temple was finished (1004 BC). The kingdom split (I Kings 12); Jeroboam reigned over 10 tribes/Israel, and Rehoboam, Solomon's son over 2 tribes/Judah.

****

(1015 BC)	*(The dating for I & II Kings is 1015 - 588 BC.)*
I Kings	
1: 5, 8, 27-39	Adonijah attempted to usurp the kingdom.
2: 1-6, 10-12	David died at age 70. He had become king at age 30 (II Sam. 5:4) and reigned 40 years. The next king was Solomon, David's son.
3: 5-15, 28	Solomon asked for wisdom (an understanding heart); God also gave him blessings for which he didn't ask.
4: 29-34	This chapter lists Solomon's princes and officers, then chapter 5 is
5: 1-18	preparation for the building of the temple.
6: 1-14, 38	The building of the house of the Lord began in the 4th year of Solomon's reign, and completed 7 years later. Verses 15 - 38 is a continuation of the building process.

I Kings continues after Song of Songs and II Chronicles 10.

****

II Chronicles (1015 - 593 BC) covers building the temple, information about the Queen of Sheba, the burning of the temple, and breaking down the walls of Jerusalem. This is the same time period as I & II Kings through chapter 24 (1015 - 610).

II Chronicles is a continuation of I Chronicles. I Chronicles ended with God's Word that David was not to build the temple and a period after the death of David.

(1015 BC)

II Chronicles

1: 1, 7-12	Solomon asked for wisdom and God's answered.
	Chapters 2 - 4 are the preparation and building of the temple.
5: 1-14	The dedication of the temple . . .
6: 5-42	God chose Jerusalem; then God's promise that Solomon would build the temple was fulfilled. Solomon's prayer . . .

****

(1014 BC)

The Song of Solomon (The Song of Songs)

Before we begin to discuss this book, I want to share what I have found. A great number of Bible readers and reference sources agree that it is a difficult task to obtain a clear understanding of the Song of Solomon. Some sources indicate this is a spiritual allegory, representing the love of Christ and His Church. That could very possibly be the theme.

Jesus taught parables speaking of things and activities relating to His earthly era so the people would better understand His teachings. Could God, in the old covenant time, have been comparing His great love for us to that of a husband and wife as that's the deepest human commitment of His people? (Ephesians 5: 31-32) As we seek Him, God allows himself to be affected by our love. (Hebrews 4: 15, Ephesians 5: 32)

There are scriptures that refer to Christ being the husband and the church being the wife such as Ephesians 5: 25-32 and Revelation 19: 7-8. In The Song of Solomon there is much detail about how a bride and bridegroom love each other and the intimacy of their relationship. Our Lord loves us so much that He wants that deep spiritual relationship with us. The Lord has put himself in the position where our love for Him brings Him pleasure. A suggestion here might be to spend some time reviewing

*New Testament scriptures relating to what Jesus went through to bring us to Himself. Praise His Holy Name! (Examples: **Matthew 26: 67, 27: 2, 12, 27, 30, 31; Luke 22: 63-64; Mark 15: 15, 19; John 19: 1-2**)*

****

(1004 BC)

II Chronicles

7: 1-4, 10-15, 19-22	Fire from heaven consumed Solomon's sacrifices - God's Glory . . . God responds with what He will do if they obey, and what He will do if they turn away from Him. In chapter 8 Solomon builds cities.

(992 BC)

9: 1-8	Queen of Sheba . . .
30-31	Solomon died and Rehoboam his son became king.

(975 BC)

10: 1, 8, 16-17	Rehoboam - 10 tribes rebelled against Rehoboam and made Jeroboam king of the 10 tribes/Israel. Rehoboam reigned in Judah. (I Kings 12: 15-17)

****

(Note for remembering whether Rehoboam or Jeroboam was Solomon's son: The one with the initial closest to the S in Solomon, Rehoboam, is Solomon's son.)

II Chronicles continued after I Kings 10, Proverbs, the end of I Kings, and Ecclesiastes.

****

(1005-992 BC)

I Kings	*(I Kings 7-11 is approximately the same time period as II Chron. 7-10)*
7: 1, 51	Information about building Solomon's house, necessary vessels, etc. for the house of the Lord is in chapter 7 and can be read by all.

(1004 BC)

I Kings	
8: 1-11,	The Ark was taken to the temple. (Oracle here means the Holy of Holies. In the New Testament it speaks of God's Word.) The Glory Cloud - In 12-21, Solomon blessed the people then he prayed to the Lord in 22-53.
54-61, 66	Solomon continued with blessings and sacrifices to God.

(992 BC)

I Kings

9: 1-5, 10-11   The Lord appeared to Solomon. Verses 6-9 is God telling what will happen if he does not obey God. The chapter ends with information about the cities Solomon built, and his navy.

10: 1-9,   The throne of David was established forever - (Joseph the husband of Mary was from the tribe of Judah and a descendant of David.) Then we can read about Solomon's great wealth and other blessings from the Lord.

(984 BC)

11: 6, 9-13,   The beginning of this chapter tells of Solomon's sins and falling away from God. His evil companions turned his heart to false gods. Verses 14 - 28 tells of God's anger and punishment. Jeroboam would be king over 10 tribes - the Northern kingdom, Israel.

29-43   Solomon died and his son Rehoboam became king of Judah which was the Southern kingdom.

****

The Book of Proverbs
(1000 - 700 BC)

The Book of Proverbs is a collection of Solomon's Godly wisdom and observations written by him under Divine inspiration. Some of the topics are as follows: trusting the Lord, moral values, chastity, thoughts, the tongue, obedience to the Lord, safety, and foolishness. As with the Book of Psalms, this book may be read at any time and not necessarily along with this Old Testament study.

Here are some scriptures you may want to memorize: Proverbs 3: 1-10, and if possible continue to memorize through verse 18; 4: 20-22; 10: 29; 11: 25, 30; 14: 21; 15: 1-2, 13; 17: 22; 18: 21; 19: 17; 26: 20; 28: 27; and 30: 4.

****

****

Ecclesiastes
The Preacher
(977 BC)
Solomon is credited with writing this book. As it is read, keep in mind the conclusion is in the last chapter (12: 11-14). The book speaks with much wisdom; however, life without The Lord is meaningless. Hope in God gives life its meaning.

The word vanity is used throughout this book which means excessive pride in ones appearance or accomplishments, useless means lacking substance or worth, foolish. Vexation is also used and is the act of annoying or irritating.

1: 1-7	Solomon speaking - vanity . . .
2: 4-5	He did all for himself.
3: 1-2, 12-13	
5: 2, 18-19	All good things come from God. Be careful what you say.
7: 5	
8: 16-17	Man can not understand all that happens in the earth. In chapters 10-11 we see that God has given man a free will and with his will he makes choices about his own life.
12: 8, 13-14	The conclusion. . .

The end of the book of Ecclesiastes
****

****

(975 BC)
I Kings

12:1-17,	After his father's death, Rehoboam sought council from the older men but did not follow their advise. God used this to divide the kingdom as He had previously spoken. (See II Chron. 10.)
19-33,	Jeroboam turned against God (forgetting God's promise to him), and promoted worship of false gods throughout all Israel. He set up an altar in Bethel and one in Dan for that worship. In the remaining chapters of this book, this is referred to as the sins of Jeroboam.

13: 1, 4-6,   A man of God was sent to prophesy against the altar that was built to the false god. The chapter continues with the man of God not fully carrying out God's instructions; he was slain.

29-34   Jeroboam continued in his sins.

****

14: 1-9,   The sins of Jeroboam continue.

15-20   This is the Lord's Word to Jeroboam because of his idol worship. The chapter continues with more about him and his son.
Nadab became king over Israel after Jeroboam's death.

21-23, 31   Rehoboam also did wickedly, and Egypt came against Judah. Rehoboam died and his son Abijam reigned in Judah.

15: 1-4, 7-16,   Asa reigned in Judah after Abijam. Then we read of Asa's death.

24   Conflict continued between Israel and Judah. (A chart of kings can be found in the appendix.)

(930 BC)
I Kings
16: 1-3,   Chapter 16 tells of more kings in Israel; Israel continued in sin and

29-33   provoked God's anger. Ahab did more to provoke the Lord to anger than all the previous kings of Israel.

****

(910 BC)
17: 1-24   God spoke through Elijah the prophet that it would not rain for 3 years. Elijah was to speak at the appointed time and it would rain.

****

18: 1-4, 7-8,

15-27,   This chapter is about Elijah and Ahab's sacrifices at Mount Carmel.

30-46   In verse 38, the fire of the Lord fell on Elijah's sacrifice. Then as God had promised, Elijah spoke and it rained.

****

(906 BC)

19: 1-2, 8-10,   Jezebel, King Ahab's evil wife, threatened Elijah. He fled. The Word of the Lord came to him. In verse 13 the Lord asked him again what he

    14- 19   was doing there, and Elijah gave him the same answer. God instructed him to do three things and told him God had 7,000 faithful servants not just one as Elijah spoke in verses 10 and 14. Elijah went his way; he found Elisha and anointed him to replace himself as God's prophet. (Elijah was instructed by God to also anoint Hazael king over Syria and Jehu king over Israel but he did not! See II Kings 8: 13, 885 BC, where Elisha heard from the Lord that Hazael was to be king over Syria and in II Kings 9: 1-3, 884 BC, where Elisha anointed Jehu king over Israel.)

                 Chapter 20 is conflict between Israel and Syria. *(The great conflicts and destruction that occurred during the following 20 + years would not have happened if Elijah had fully obeyed The Lord.)*

21: 1-4, 7, 14,   Jezebel obtained the vineyard by her wicked ways.

    27-29   Ahab humbled himself before the Lord.

(897 BC)

22: 37, 40,   Here we read of a battle between Israel (King Ahab) and Syria.

    51-53   Ahab's son, Ahaziah reigned over Israel. He served Baal and provoked God's anger.

The end of the book of I Kings
****

****

(974 BC)

II Chronicles

11: 4-5   God told them not to fight against each other.

12: 1-4, 7, 12, 15-16

(957 BC)

13: 1   Abajiah was king of Judah.

14: 1-2, 8-12   Asa was the next king of Judah and the Lord fought for Asa.

15: 1-2,   God spoke through Azariah the Prophet to seek The Lord.
   9-12, 19

16: 9, 13   When Israel came against Judah, Asa began to trust surrounding nations for help instead of seeking God.

****

(912 BC)
II Chronicles

17: 1-12   Asa's son Jehoshaphat reigned in Judah. God blessed him.

(897BC)
II Chronicles

18: 34   Ahab was king of Israel and died in battle. In Chapter 19, Jehoshaphat instructed the people of Judah to serve the Lord.

20: 1, 3-4,   This chapter records the enemy coming against them then Jehoshaphat
   14-17,   and all Judah sought direction from the Lord.
   20-25   Seeking the Lord . . .

21: 1,   Jehosophat's son, Jehoram reigned in Judah. He did evil.
   6-7, 10,   God's punishment on Jehoram is noted in verses 11 - 19.
   20   This chapter ends with the death of King Jehoram.

II Chronicles

22: 2-3, 13   Ahaziah the next king of Judah did evil. His father, Jehoram, was the former king of Judah. Jehoram, Ahab's son, was then king of Israel. Jehoram and Joram are the same name. (Israel also had a king Ahaziah. See the Kings Chart in appendix)

II Chronicles continues after II Kings 12

****

(896 - 588 BC)
II Kings   *Note: Babylon was in power from 612 - 538 BC.*

II Kings 1: 1-6, 9-18	King Ahaziah (Ahab's son) of Israel desired a word from Baalzebub the god of Ekron. His messengers didn't go there; on the way, they met Elijah who gave them a word from Almighty God for Ahaziah. *(Ahaziah considered Elijah his enemy. Elijah had called fire down from Heaven upon Ahaziah's messengers. That was under the Old Covenant. Under the New Covenant, Jesus paid the price for sins and has made another way. God does not exercise His wrath on people like He did in that time. In our day, what appears at times to be God's wrath is the consequences of man's sins. Not obeying Almighty God opens one up to the works of the devil. Satan can destroy! See Luke 9: 52-56; Jesus wouldn't allow His disciples to call fire down as Elijah did.)*
2: 1-22	Elijah & Elisha - *(Elisha requested a double portion of Elijah's spirit. That was Old Covenant. Since Jesus came we are under the New Covenant and we can't get a double portion of someone's spirit. All believers have the fullness of God in their spirit. It's up to each believer to seek God, study the Word, and learn how to release God's power by faith. Romans 10:17 tells us faith comes by hearing the Word.)*
(895 BC) II Kings 3: 1-7, 16-17, 20, 24	They went to battle and there was no water. Elisha was sought and God used him to provide water, then delivered Moab into their hands.
4: 1-2, 7, 17, 35, 41-44	This chapter is details of miracles performed through Elisha and may be read by all.
5: 1, 27	In verses 1-19, God used Elisha to cleanse Naaman of leprosy. Verses 20 - 27 record how Elisha's servant, Gehazi, followed after Naaman and collected a reward for the miracle. He attempted to deceive Elisha by lying to him. Gehazi was punished. The details may be read by all.

(893 BC)

II Kings

6: 4-7   The sons of the prophets were cutting down trees to build a house. An axe fell into the water and Elisha made it swim. The chapter continues with God performing miracles through Elisha; the Syrian army was blinded, and a famine arose in Samaria.

****

(892 BC)

Chapter 7   God sent relief to Samaria and the attackers, the Syrians, fled. One of the high officers of Samaria, who had been appointed by the King, disbelieved that they were all gone; he was killed in the end of the conflict.

(885 - 884 BC)

II Kings

8:1-7, 12,   Hazael reigned in Syria after Benhadad.
16-19,   Judah did evil, but was not destroyed because of God's promise to
24-27   David.

9: 1-7, 13,   Elisha appointed a son of the prophets to anoint Jehu, son of Jehoshaphat, king over Israel. He was anointed to destroy the whole house of Ahab. (See I Kings 19: 15-16 where Elijah was called to do this, but he did not.) The chapter continues with prophesy of what will happen to Jezebel, war against the house of Ahab, and Jezebel's death as had been prophesied.

****

10: 10-11,   In Chapter 10, Jehu destroyed Ahab's sons and all his kindred in Jezreel
21, 25-31   and Samaria. He pretended zeal for the worship of Baal in order to entice all the worshippers of Baal to gather together - then he destroyed them (25-28). However, he did not depart from the sins of Jeroboam. He died and the next king over Israel, in Samaria, was Jehoahaz. Verses 32-33 tell of Hazael's (Syria) victories according to God's plan.

11: 1-4, 8,   Chapter 11 is about Judah. Athaliah was the daughter of King Ahab
12-21   of Israel and the wife of King Jehoram of Judah. (*The name Joram is the same person as Jehoram. Jehoiada was the priest.*) Athaliah reigned as Queen until Joash, son of Ahaziah, became king at age 7. He was not the son of Queen Athaliah.

(878 BC)

II Kings

12: 1-21   Jehoash/Joash reigned over Judah and Jehu was king in Israel. The breaches that were in the House of The Lord were repaired and the King of Syria went up against Jerusalem. Jehoash paid him off with treasures from the House of the Lord, then he went away. In verse 20, we see that Amaziah his son became the next king of Judah.

****

(II Kings continues to follow the lineage of the kings of Judah and Israel and describes the conflict with each other and surrounding areas. Israel did much evil in the sight of the Lord; however, when a king would repent, God had mercy. Judah also sinned against God at times; the Lord preserved that nation because of His promise to David. Both Israel and Judah had a king named Joash also called Jehoash, and kings named Ahaziah as noted in the appendix.)

(856 BC)

II Kings

13: 1-6,   This tells of Israel's struggles with Syria. Elisha's last prophesy is
    10-13,   recorded in verses 14-19, then he died.
    20 -25

14: 1-3,   This records the struggles between the kings of Judah and Israel.
    15-21,   It may be read in it's entirety.
    27-29

     (Chapters 15 and 16 are more about kings that reigned in Israel and Judah. See the appendix chart for a list of Judah and Israel's kings.)

****

15: 1-4,   Idol worship continued; struggles with Assyria can be seen in the
    7-10, 19,   verses listed.
    22, 29

16: 1-2, 20   King Ahaz reigned in Judah; he didn't fully follow the Lord but walked in the ways of the kings of Israel. This chapter also records issues with the Syrians.

(721 BC)
II Kings

17: 6-8, 18   Chapter 17 returns to telling about Israel's kings. It records rebellion and disobedience of Israel's hardened hearts, Assyria carrying the people of Israel away, and populating cities of Israel with men from other lands. We can see in verse 24 they possessed Samaria and also dwelt in other cities of Israel. Israel continued to serve the graven images instead of the Lord.

(This was the beginning of the exile of God's people (those in Israel) into the Babylonian empire. We can see in the following chapters that King Hezekiah of Judah would not submit to the king of Assyria.)

18: 1-6, 9-11,   Hezekiah reigned over Judah in Jerusalem and served God.

17, 19   Rabshakeh was sent by King Sennacherib of Assyria to speak to Hezekiah about Jerusalem and Judah. This chapter continues with Rabshakeh's blasphemy of the Almighty God.

19: 1-2,   Chapter 19 is a continuation of 18; it is messages between the
5-6, 19   arrogant king of Assyria and the Lord speaking through Isaiah and Hezekiah's messengers.

32-37   Hezekiah prayed; the Lord responded to his supplication.

****

(713 BC)
II Kings

20: 1-3, 6,   Hezekiah was sick and prayed he would not die as Isaiah the prophet had spoken (Isaiah 38). God answered his prayer with 15 more years of life. *(Hezekiah would not accept the Word of the Lord that he was to die. God answered his prayer, and during the 15 years granted to him his son Manasseh was born; see verse 21. Manasseh is recorded as being the most evil king of Judah.)*

16-18   Isaiah prophesied, to King Hezekiah of Judah, regarding the upcoming Babylonian captivity of Judah.

(698 BC)

21: 1-2,	In Judah, Manasseh, Hezekiah's son reigned; he did evil then his son,
11-12,	Amon, followed in his evil ways.
18-24	

(641 BC)

22: 1-20   King Josiah was Amon's son.

****

(624 BC)

II Kings

23: 1-3, 25,	Chapter 23: 1-24 gives detail of what King Josiah did to remove the
29-37	idols and abominable practices from Judah. Josiah served the Lord with
	all his heart, soul, and might. Evil kings succeeded him.

(Prophesies regarding the Babylonian captivity of the Jews were given long before the events took place. Babylon was in power from 612 to 538 BC. Jerusalem/Judah's captivity was completed in 586 BC; Israel's captivity began years before Judah's. The Scriptures refer to Israel and Jerusalem being besieged which means to surround with hostile forces, over time, in an attempt to capture; Jerusalem was besieged 20 years.)

Persia conquered the Babylonians and from 538 - 333 BC Persia was in power. The restoration of the Jews, under King Cyrus of Persia, began in 538 BC. The decree went out in the first year of his reign, Ezra 1: 1-3, continuing until ~ 400 BC. Released captives returned under one nation, Israel. They were not split anymore. However; all did not return, some stayed in Babylon and others settled in surrounding areas.)

(610 BC)

II Kings

| 24: 1-3, | King Nebuchadnezzar of Babylon besieged Jerusalem. This was Isaiah |
| 10-17 | and Huldah's prophesies coming to pass. |

(588 BC)

25: 1-3,	Jerusalem was besieged in the 9th year of Nebuchadnezzar's reign.
8-13,	In the 19th year the Temple and other houses were burned, and the walls
	of the city broken down.

22-30   Gedaliah was made ruler in Judah by Nebuchadnezzar who was slain. After the death of Nebuchadnezzar, the new king of Babylon showed King Jehoiachin of Judah favor, and released him from prison.

(Verse 1 of chapter 25 is in the ninth year of Nebuchadnezzar's reign, verse 8 is the nineteenth year, and verse 27 is the first year of Evilmerodach's reign in Babylon. The captivity was a process starting with Israel; some sources state Israel was first besieged as early as 721. The captivity and carrying away of Israel and Judah was completed by ~586 BC.)

The end of the book of II Kings
****

****

(878 BC)
II Chronicles
23: 11, 16   Joash the son of Ahaziah - Jehoiada the priest . . .
24: 1-2,   Joash . . .
   17-18, 27

(870 - 732 BC) Possible time for Psalms 46, 50, 82, 83, and 115. See more references to Psalms after the book of Daniel.

****

Jonah
(862 BC)
Jonah
1: 1- 6,   The Lord spoke to Jonah and he disobeyed. God responded.
   9-12,   Jonah spoke to the shipmaster.
   15-17   The Lord was in charge of Jonah's current circumstances.
2: 1, 10   In chapter 2, we can find Jonah's prayer, and the Lord's response.

3: 1-2, 4-6, This is Jonah's mission to Nineveh.
   9-10

4: 1, 11   Next we see Jonah's response to God's mercy, and God's reply to Jonah.

The end of the book of Jonah

****

****

(827 BC)

II Chronicles

25: 1-2,   Amaziah succeeded Joash in Jerusalem, and fought against Joash of
14-15,   Israel. After obeying God for a time, he won the battle against Edom,
28   and turned away from the Lord.

26: 1-4   Uzziah, Amaziah's son, did that which was right in God's sight until his
16-21   heart became proud.
            (God hates pride. See Prov. 8:13, 11: 2, Isa. 14: 12-15 and many more.)

27: 6   This narrative of Judah's kings continues with Jotham then in chapter
            28, Ahaz became king.

(741 BC)

II Chronicles

28: 1-2, 22, 24

29: 1-8,   The next King was Hezekiah who had the temple cleansed.
35-36

30: 21,   Chapter 30 continues with Hezekiah . . . Some children of Israel were
            present when the Passover was observed.

26-27

****

(726 BC)

II Chronicles

31: 1-2, 21   This is a continuation of the previous chapter.

32: 1, 13-15, Sennacherib of Assyria planned to fight against Jerusalem. He talked
22-23   against Almighty God. The Lord saved Hezekiah and all Jerusalem.
               Chapter 33 tells of Manasseh's wicked reign.

(641 BC)

34: 1-2, 15,   King Josiah followed the Lord. Hilkiah was the high priest.
    19, 33

(623 BC)

II Chronicles

35: 18-19   Under Josiah's reign the Passover was again observed.

(593 BC)

36: 1-9,   Josiah's son, Jehoahaz/Jehoiakim reigned 3 months in Jerusalem then
    11-12,   Jehoiachin. Next was Jedekiah. The people of Jerusalem refused to
    14-20,   turn to the Lord, and Jerusalem was destroyed.
    22-23   Verses 22-23 would be dated ~538 BC. Compare this to the text in Ezra
    1: 1-3. Isaiah prophesied of this in 712 BC (Isaiah 44:28).

God stirred the heart of King Cyrus of Persia to fulfill the prophesy of Isaiah and Jeremiah regarding the return of the Jews from captivity to rebuild the Temple. This occurred under King Cyrus (~538 BC) in the first year of Persia being in power over the Babylonian Empire.

The end of the book of II Chronicles

****

****

The Book of Joel is a "near" and "far" prophesy. There are other near and far prophesies in the Old Testament as well. The prophesied calamities in this book came on the people being prophesied to at that time. The far prophesy was regarding the coming of the Messiah and the Holy Spirit which occurred with the New Covenant, and also was concerning the final end time coming of the Lord. Jerusalem will be inhabited forever, salvation will come out from thence, and whosoever shall call upon the name of the Lord shall be saved. This relates to the new covenant and the time of the Lord Jesus Christ, the Messiah.

(~800 BC)

Joel

1: 13-15   The day of the Lord is at hand.

2: 1-2, 11-13, Joel declared God's judgment is coming. Turn back to the Lord.

21-32	He continued the prophesy regarding end times, and spoke of the coming of the Holy Spirit. (See Acts 2.)
3: 14-18	All will know that He is God.

The end of the book of Joel

****

****

The Book of Amos

God is speaking again, now through Amos, His judgment against Damascus (capital city of Syria), Philistia, Gaza, Tyrus/Tyre, Edom, and Ammon in chapter 1. Continuing in chapter 2 is judgment of Moab, Judah, and Israel. God was reminding Israel of all He had done for them in the past. Next is His rebuke, then description of Israel's punishment to come. They had turned away from God, and were sinning against Him. Chapter 3 and the beginning of 4 continue regarding Israel and Samaria.

(787 BC)
Amos

4: 7, 12-13	Israel is being reminded that God had previously brought punishment on them and they didn't repent. Judgment is coming . . .
5: 4-8, 12-15 18-20 26-27	This is a call to return to the Lord. He is omniscient and knows how terrible their sins are. The Day of the Lord . . .
6: 3, 8, 14	The people of Israel refused to admit the day of disaster is coming. Chapter 7 begins Amos' visions from the Lord. He prophesied against King Jeroboam of Israel. Israel will be taken away into exile.
8: 7-12	The visions continue in chapter 8 - Punishment is coming upon Israel. There will be hunger for a message from the Lord.
9: 8-15	God will not destroy all the descendants of Jacob; the kingdom of David will be restored. In that day . . . blessings.

The end of the book of Amos

****

****

Hosea
(785 - 725 BC)
Hosea

1: 1-10	God speaks through Hosea comparing Israel and Judah to an unfaithful wife. (Jezreel means what God planted.)
3: 5	The symbolic representations continue through chapter 2 and beyond.
4: 1, 6	There are also encouraging inserts of what will come after the
5: 15	judgment of their sinful behaviors. **(2: 23, 3: 5)**
6: 4	Then, in chapters 7- 11 there is more rebuke of Israel in graphic language and 12 speaks judgment against Judah.
13: 4-9	
14: 1-2, 4, 9	This is God's call to return to Him and His mercy. Calves in verse 2 (KJV) means thanks.

The end of the book of Hosea
****

****************************`

*(**Before we begin Isaiah, it's important to remember that the chapters are not in chronological order is this book.** It's also somewhat difficult to understand due to the symbolic language at times and the numerous names of places and nations. Some notes are provided to fill in a portion of the information needed to have a better understanding of where it took place, and what nations certain people belonged to.*

Isaiah prophesied during the reigns of 3 kings of Judah. These prophesies by Isaiah regarding the upcoming captivity are also recorded in Micah, Nahum, and II Kings. Descriptive language is used by Isaiah to define the sins of Israel that provoked God to anger. Many of the chapters in Isaiah contain prophesies about times yet to come.)

(760 - 698 BC)
Isaiah

1: 1, 16-20, 26-28	Cease from evil and turn back to the Lord. The Lord continues to speak through Isaiah in descriptive language concerning judgment of their sins and reconciliation.

2: 1-5, 12	The Word of the Lord came to Isaiah regarding the last days. **(2: 3-4)** Verses 13 - 22 are words against the rebellious and disobedient people. The Word of the Lord to Judah and Jerusalem through Isaiah continues in chapter 3.
3: 8-11	There is a reward for the righteous but woe unto the wicked.

****

Isaiah

4: 2-3	The Branch is Jesus - Chapter 4 continues with blessings to the obedient ones.
(760 BC)	
5: 13, 20-21	Chapter 5 begins with a metaphor; the vineyard is the Jews. The Lord gave His people prosperity yet they rebelled and served false gods. Therefore means this is a continuation of what was just written. He speaks of God's punishment on the wicked and going into captivity.
6: 1-8	Jotham was king at that time. This was Isaiah's vision of the Lord on His throne and Isaiah's response which was a humbled and repentant heart. (You may want to memorize Isa. 6: 1-3)
7: 1-7,	Chapter 7 begins by telling of war with surrounding nations - Ahaz was king of Judah.
10-14, 17	Isaiah prophesied of Jesus; God with us/Immanuel **(7: 14-16)**. A conspiracy of Syria and Israel against Judah fails; the narrative continues through to the end of chapter 7.

****

Isaiah

8:1, 13-14, 19-20	The King of Assyria is coming. Mahershalalhashbaz is a word that was given to the prophet by divine direction and means that Damascus and Samaria are soon to be plundered by the king of Assyria. Seek God and not evil spirits.
(771 BC)	
9: 2, 6-7,	Again the coming of Jesus was prophesied; a light is coming to the Gentiles.

9-10   The end of chapter 9 tells of judgment coming against Israel because of their pride, wickedness, and defiance.

****

Micah (750 - 710 BC)

Micah

1: 1, 2, 5-6, 9   Micah was from Moresa a city in Judah. He received a Word from the Lord for Samaria and Judah. Then came the Lord's witness against Judah and Israel, and the foretelling of calamities coming against them.

2: 1, 12-13   Woe to the evildoers. Chapter 2 continues with prophesy of the upcoming captivity of the 10 tribes, and their return.

                 Bozrah was the chief city in Edom (Gen. 36: 33). Edom has already been explained in this study. Jacob's brother Esau had his name changed to Edom in Gen. 25: 29 - 34. Edom, which is also Mt. Seir, is the country settled by his descendants. The New Testament/Greek name for Edom is Idumea (Mk. 3: 8).

                 Chapter 3 is an inditement against Judah and Israel, proclaiming they will be the reason Jerusalem shall be destroyed.

4: 1-7   In the last days . . . peace and glory. (halted - uncertain or hesitant)

<u>5:2</u>   The Messiah to come (He came) from Bethlehem.

Micah

6: 1-8   Chapters 6-7 tell of God's controversy with His people including a

7: 18-20   description of their sins. The prophesy ends with God's promise of mercy.

The end of the book of Micah

****

****

Nahum

(All the people, including the king of Nineveh, repented under the preaching of Jonah. Nahum came to Nineveh about 150 years later to find the city had become totally godless. God gave him this vision foretelling the destruction of Nineveh which was the capital of the Assyrian Empire.)

(713 BC)
Nahum

1: 1-3, 6-8, 15   The Lord will not leave the guilty unpunished.
God used Assyria to chastise His people Israel for their sins. Then, He would punish Assyria's sins.

Chapters 2 and 3 tell, in expressive language, that Nineveh will fall for their multitude of great sins. Further information on these two chapters can be found in a note in the Amplified Bible.

3: 7, 18 -19   Assyria will be utterly destroyed. (In 19, bruit means news or rumor.)

The end of the book of Nahum
****

(713 BC)
Isaiah
10: 1-3, 5,
12-13,
20-23,
27   Chapter 10 is judgment against those who make unjust decrees.
God will use Assyria against the evildoers (prideful idol worship) in Jerusalem, then there will be judgment against Assyria for their arrogance and evil plans. God encourages His people. (The word consumption in verses 22 & 23 of the KJV means completion.)
In verses 28-34, Isaiah speaks God's Word that in the end the enemy will be destroyed.

(713 BC)
Isaiah

<u>11: 1-10</u>   These verses speak of the first and second coming of Christ. Remember Almighty God has been preserving a path of appropriate ancestors for His Son, Messiah Jesus. Root of Jesse in Verse 10 means descendant; Jesse was the father of King David. Scriptures tell us in prophesies from

Almighty God that the Messiah will come from the tribe of Judah and the house of David. The rest of chapter 11 gives details.

12: 1-6   In that day . . .

****

(712 BC)

Isaiah

13: 6, 9-13,   This is Isaiah's vision regarding the day of the Lord's wrath.
   19-22

God's wrath will come, in the time of the great tribulation, against the wickedness of those who have rebelled against Almighty God. The chapter ends with details of that great destruction. *(It has been explained at another point in this study that the righteous, the followers of Jesus, will be delivered from God's wrath.)*

14: 1-5,   This appears to be referring to the restoration of Israel from their captivity in Babylon.

  12-17,   Then, it moves on to what is going to happen to the devil in the end. He originally was named Lucifer and fell from God's grace by declaring that he would be like God. He has been the instigator of the wickedness and evil that has occurred in the earth. That will all end with Jesus' second coming.

  24-27   Verse 27 ends in a question and the answer is obvious - no one.

Isaiah chapters 15 and 16 are one prophesy against Moab, places East of the Dead Sea, and clouds of war rising from Assyria. They were idol worshippers and Moab was destroyed in 711 BC. Information on the many places mentioned in these chapters can be found in the appendix.

15: 1   The burden of Moab continues through chapters 15 and 16.

16: 6, 10,

  12-14   It shall come to pass . . .

Isaiah

17: 1-3, 14   This describes Assyria's threatening's against Syria and Israel.

(Nineveh was the capital of Assyria. Aroer was a name covering an area of several places on the north bank of the Arnon River east of the Dead Sea. The Arnon River formed the boundary between Moab and Ammon. Damascus, in Syria, is the oldest city known to history. God will destroy Assyria in the end. The Assyrians were known to be very cruel people and the sin that continued to provoke God's anger was idol worship.)

Isaiah 18 is an obscure prophesy possibly not only regarding Ethiopia, but the Jews who resided there. (Ethiopia was also called Cush and was south of Egypt.)

****

Isaiah

19: 1-4,	Prophesy concerning Egypt - They will fight against each other in a civil war within Egypt.
5-6,	This prediction regarding the waters has come to pass.
11-13, 17,	*(Zoan was a town on the east bank of the Nile River in Egypt; Noph was in Egypt on the west bank of the Nile.)* Judah will be a terror unto the Egyptians. Verses 18 - 23 are a future conversion of Egypt. Verse 21 states in that day the Egyptians will know the Lord.
19: 23-25	The chapter continues with in that day. . . a future time . . . the Day of The Lord.

(714 BC)

Isaiah

Chapter 20 is a prophesy against Egypt and Ethiopia. Isaiah was to be a sign to them of their coming captivity by the dreaded Assyrians. They were a nation that was known for disgracing their conquered people.

Chapter 21 is a prediction regarding Babylon and surrounding areas being conquered by the Medes and Persians.

21: 3, 9	The power of God's visions caused adverse physical effects at times in the prophets as seen in Daniel and Isaiah. Verse 9 - Babylon has fallen, then there are more descriptive details throughout this chapter.
22: 1-11,	The Valley of vision is Jerusalem. Chapter 22 describes the preparation in Jerusalem against an attack of Assyria. Among other preparations, they diverted the water to the Pool of Salom so Jerusalem would have

water in a time of attack. They tried to prepare in their own strength without looking to God.

20-24   In that day . . . This chapter had an immediate and a far fulfillment. The far is yet to come. (There were 6 other Eliakim's mentioned in Scripture.) This Eliakim was over the household of King Hezekiah of Judah as a servant (II Kings 18:18 & Isaiah 36:3). He is referred to as a type of Christ.

****

23: 1, 5   This is judgment against Tyre, a Phoenician seaport. (Nebuchadnezzar captured Tyre 13 years later.) The chapter continues in Isaiah's difficult to understand language.

(712 BC)
Isaiah

24: 14, 23   Chapter 24 tells of dreadful judgments that are to occur before the Kingdom Age commences in the latter days.
The Lord shall reign.

25: 1, 4, 8-9   Past declarations by the prophets shall be fulfilled in God's timing.

26: **1-4**,   In that day . . . (Isa. 26: 3-4)

   7-9,   Reward for the just -

  12-14   Other leaders have died but You are God.
The glorious hope of the coming Great Day of the Lord is mingled here with discourse on the punishment of the wicked (unsaved).

Isaiah

27: 1-3,   This tells of destruction of the enemies of the Lord and God's care of His children. Dark red wine was more valuable. This parable of a vineyard refers to how God values His children.

  12-13   Gathering of the children of Israel . . .

****

Isaiah 28

28: 1, 5   Isaiah is speaking to Samaria, the Northern Kingdom, regarding the approaching ruin of the Israelites, but he speaks to Judah & Benjamin favorably.

28: 16   The coming of Jesus is prophesied.
(712 BC)

29: 1,   Ariel here means lion of God and is a poetic name for Jerusalem. The
   18-24   chapter begins with foretelling of the siege of Jerusalem.
                 Chapters 29 - 33 all refer to the invasion of Sennacherib, great distress
                 it caused the Jews, and God's unexpected deliverance. In that day . . . A
                 glorious day is coming.

30: 1-2,   Cover with a covering in verse 1 means to ratify a covenant. The Lord
                 spoke of punishment for their lack of trust in God. At one point they
                 chose to look to Egypt for help instead of to the Lord, then we can see
                 God's wrath for forsaking Him.
   4-13,   Isaiah prophesies much regarding God's response to evil, but The Lord
   15-16,   always showed His mercy when His people repented and turned back
   18-21   to Him. Be still and trust God. The chapter continues with His wrath
                 toward the wicked.

31: 1-3   In chapter 31, the Jews are reproved again for confiding in Egypt instead
                 of God.

*(Judah, the Southern kingdom, did not rebel as much or often as Israel, the Northern
kingdom, did. Samaria was the capitol city of Israel and Jerusalem the capitol of Judah.)*

32: 1, **15-18**   The kingdom of righteousness is coming.

****
33: 5   Foretelling of judgment and righteousness continues throughout 33.
34: 1-2, 8,   (Vengeance means punishment in return for wrong, recompense
                 deserving, and controversy is strife or anger aroused by something
                 unjust.)
   16   Seek the Book of the Lord.
Isaiah
35: 1-6,   Prophesy (713 BC) and fulfillment (31 AD); see Matthew 11: 2-5,
   10   everlasting joy. . . yet to come.

Chapters 36 and 37 are one dissertation.

36: 1-5,   Sennacherib, king of Assyria, threatened Judah throughout this whole
13-15, 18 chapter. Assyrian pride . . . Rabshakeh's blasphemy of the Lord . . .

37: 1-2, 5-7, Continued from Chapter 36 - The details of the conflict can be read in
this chapter. King Hezekiah went into the House of The Lord and
14-20,   prayed to Almighty God. His servants went to Isaiah the Prophet to get
33-38   a Word from The Lord. (Nineveh was the capitol city of Assyria.)
Sennacherib was slain.

(713 BC)

38: 1-8, 21   King Hezekiah of Judah was sick; he prayed and the Lord answered (II
Kings 20). Then came God's healing through Isaiah.

****

39: 1-8   Hezekiah showed all his treasures to the representatives of the king
of Babylon - pride in his own accomplishments. The Lord spoke to him
through Isaiah.

(Chapter 40 and forward is a message of comfort for God's people, a time of favor, Israel's deliverance, and return to their own land. The message continues with a promise of the coming Messiah, His second coming and God's plan for our future.)

40: 1-5, 8,   **Verse 3** was fulfilled with John the Baptist. The Word of God is sure.
10-14,   Verses 10 - 31 are Scriptures regarding God's greatness. **(40: 10-11)**
17-18,
21-22,
25-26,   Here are more verses suggested for memorizing:
28-31

Isa. 40: 8, 28-29, 31; 41: 10; 44: 3-4; and 48:17.

41: 8-16   The descendants of Abraham, the tribe of Jacob, were chosen by God
to be ancestors of Jesus. The chapter continues with promises of God's
everlasting love and blessings. **(41: 15-16)**

****

42: 1-9   This is a prophesy of the coming Messiah; Jesus fulfilled this part and He will return. He brought salvation for all including the Gentiles (Acts 10). The prisoners in verse 7 refer to the Old Testament believers. Then we can read about God's goodness, righteousness, and anger against sin.

43: 1-19,   Chapter 43 is a continuation of the previous chapter. It tells of God's
    25   promises to Israel and Judah because He loves them. Then in 16-19, He exhorts them to remember His miracles of deliverance and care in the past; He is now going to do a new thing.
               Even though they did not honor God . . .

****

(712 BC)
Isaiah

44: 1-8,   God's blessings - In verse 2, Jesurun refers to the people of Israel. Verse 9 begins a declaration of the futility of idols.

    28   This is a prophesy about Cyrus, King of Persia, sending God's people back to Jerusalem to rebuild after their captivity in Babylon. Persia would conquer Babylon thus Nebuchadnezzar would not be in control in that future time. God spoke this through Isaiah more than 150 years before Cyrus was born and even spoke his name. Judah was taken into captivity in 586 BC. *(There is information regarding the fulfillment of this prophesy in a note between chapters 5 and 6 of Daniel.)*

45: 1-25   The prophesy about Cyrus continues. Verse 11 is a rebuke in the form of a question. The chapter ends by declaring God's omnipotence.

46: 9-13   Verses 1-8 tell that idols were carried but God carries His people. The ravenous bird is Cyrus who is the man God declared would send men to rebuild the Temple in Jerusalem.

               Chapter 47 tells of God allowing the Chaldeans to conquer His people, but continues with judgment on Babylon. The false gods of the Chaldeans, can't save them. Verses 12 and 13 name them as sorcerers, astrologers, star-gazers, and monthly prognosticators. Even though

God allowed them to conquer Israel and Judah, the Chaldeans will be overcome.

48: 1-13,	He will not give His glory to anyone else. God explains that He speaks through His prophets before events come to pass so no one can claim their false gods brought to pass certain happenings.
17, 20, 22	It is God that teaches His people to profit. He redeemed His people; there is no peace for the wicked.

49: 13	Isaiah 49 - 50 are obscure at times; however, certain themes are evident. First, The Messiah, Jesus, will come and be a light to the Gentiles as well as to the Jews **(49: 7-10)** - God's mercy. There are also exhortations to trust in Christ. In verse 26 of chapter 49, the Lord exclaims that all shall know that He is the only Lord, Savior, and Redeemer. He is the mighty One of Jacob.

50: 6	This chapter is a foretelling of the scourging of Jesus before the crucifixion.

****

(Zion is the South West hill of Jerusalem - the older and higher part of Jerusalem often referred to as the City of David. Jerusalem was the city where God chose to put His name. See I Kings 11: 36. Jerusalem was originally an Amorite city and all the nations that occupied the city at different times are listed in the concordance.)

(712 BC)
Isaiah

51: 1-7, 10-11,	This chapter begins with comfort and encouragement for the righteous.
15-16	He is God who dried up the Red Sea for the Israelites escape from Egypt, and He will also bring to pass His everlasting promises. Israel's enemies will become the afflicted.

52: 1-10,	In that day. . . *(A reference for v. 1 is Revelation 21: 27; in v. 2 daughter means descendant, and captive is one taken away captive.)*

13-15	The chapter ends with Almighty God speaking about Jesus as His servant. At times in previous chapters, God spoke through Isaiah regarding the deliverance of the Jews from the captivity of Babylon, hope for the Gentiles, and the ultimate deliverance of mankind from sin and death. From this point forward to chapter 57, the message is regarding the Messiah.

(712 BC)

53: 1-12	This chapter can be studied with the fulfillment in the New Testament. (33 AD - Jn. 1: 1-14; Mt. 26: 67, Mt. 27-31, 57-58; Lk. 23: 34) Time and meditation on these verses would be time well spent. He did all that for me and for you!

54: 7-10, 13-17	This is speaking to the righteous Gentiles as well as the Jews. These are memory suggestions: Isa. 53: 4-5 and 54: 13-15, 17.

****

55: 5-13	God's spoken Word will come to pass.
56: 1, 4-8	That day of everlasting salvation in near. Choose pleasing God. Jesus spoke of the Lord's house as a house of prayer for all people - Luke 19: 46.

(698 BC)
Isaiah

57: 3-5, 15, 20-21	Here is a cry to the wicked.
58: 1-4,	These verses are about outward ceremonial fasting and prayer that is not acceptable to the Lord.
6-10	This is the fast that is acceptable to the Lord.

59: 1-2, 12-13, **20-21**	A rebuke for evil doings is followed by a description of their sins. The Lord's response . . .

****

60: 1-3, 14,   The imagery in this chapter speaks of the period of time after the Jews and Gentiles become one fold with one Shepherd. The one fold is all the believers in Jesus, and the time mentioned here also includes a time that has not yet come. That time shall follow a time of gross darkness.

19-22   The Kingdom age has great blessings for God's people.

61: 1-3,   The coming Messiah - This was fulfilled as Jesus read from the scrolls in
10-11   Luke 4: 18-19. However, He stopped at verse 3 because it continues with speaking of the Kingdom Age. The Old Testament prophets did not understand there would be two comings of the Messiah thus prophesies of the two ages were merged together.

Isaiah
62: 1-3,   Next is the restoration of Israel.
11-12

(There are many Scriptures throughout the Bible that use things, customs, and peoples of their times to describe other events. This was obviously intended to provide a better understanding of the meaning and purpose of the messages from Almighty God.)

63:1-9   Before that restoration, there will be great tribulation. Edom/Mt Seir is the country settled by Esau's descendants/Edomites. They were always idolaters. The ancient capital city was Bozrah; Ezion-geber and Sela were the seaports. These were prototypes of what was to come. The Messiah's garments were stained with blood and He is mighty to save.

     Verses 3 - 4 of Isaiah chapter 63 are the answer to the questions in verses 1 and 2. It appears that He is comparing the Edomites to His enemies in the end times. The Lord will crush the antichrist and all of the Lord's enemies like grapes in a winepress and there is no one to help - it's all God. No one can assist in His atonement.

     The red is blood - see Rev.14: 19-20 and 19: 13-16. The wine-press is the wrath of God. The fierceness of God's wrath will usher in the Glorious Kingdom age.

He was their Savior in times of old and He will be our Savior till the end - forever.

Verses 9 through 14 are remembering Israel's disobedience, God's graciousness, and His glorious arm of restoration. Verses 15 through 19 are a prayer. This appeal to God continues in the following chapter.

64: 4, 6, 8,   Part of this prayer is repeated in I Corinthians 2: 9. The prayer is one of repentance and declaring God's greatness. They admitted their sins instead of trying to justify their actions before God.

Isaiah
65: 1-5, 9,   God's answer is that when His people rebelled, He reached out to the Gentiles (See Romans 9: 22-24). God will gather His servants from Israel; verse 15 tells us He will call the servants of God by another name. Is that new name Christian and/or His Church?

17-19,   This is a far prophesy about the Kingdom Age and continues to the end
24-25   of the chapter.

(698 BC)
Isaiah
66: 1-2,   The Lord is speaking of the temple that was rebuilt and His thoughts
13-14,   about it. How can you build a house for Me? Heaven is my throne
18,   and the earth is my footstool - I created it all!
22-24   God is not going to stop fulfilling His promises. All nations will see His glory. Verse 24 describes hell and those who chose to go there by rebelling against the Lord (also in Mark 9: 44 - 48; & Luke 16: 23, 26).

The end of the book of Isaiah
****

****

Zephaniah

(630 BC)

Zephaniah

1: 1, 4-6, 7-8, **14-18**	Zephaniah prophesied against Judah and Israel. The following prophesies appear to be near and far prophesies. This is to be applied to their present circumstances as well as a time in the far future. All Israel was to be carried off into captivity, and then it speaks of Jesus' second coming.
2: 1-7	God's anger against the sins of the nations - A cry to seek the Lord . . . The Lord is speaking through the Prophet for Judah, Israel, and all nations to turn from evil and seek Him. The chapter continues with judgment against the pride of surrounding nations.
3: 1-20	God's judgment continues, then He promises blessings for His obedient people with a promise of a pure language and peace. The Lord will rejoice! Another memory verse is 3: 17.

The end of the book of Zephaniah
****

The wrath of God will not be poured out until the end of the age. His people, those who believe in the Messiah, Jesus Christ, will be delivered from God's wrath. The second coming of Jesus is yet to come, Acts 1: 11, and that is the time period when His wrath will be poured out. Believers have His Word that He will come again, and we are free from the wrath to come. He will take believers away to be with Him before His wrath is poured out. (See I Thessalonians 1:10, 4: 16-18 & 5: 9, Romans 5: 8-9 as well as other scriptures. This could be a study in itself.)

****

Habakkuk

According to the dates, Habakkuk would be in order after Jeremiah 3. Chapter 3 is dated 629 BC and chapter 4 is dated 612 BC. Israel had already fallen.

(626 BC)

Habakkuk

1: 1 -8,	Habakkuk cried out to Almighty God regarding the violence and wickedness he sees all around him. God answers - God will use the Chaldeans/Babylonians against sinful Judah. In 12 - 17 Habakkuk
12-13	complains to God again. God's answer is in the next chapter.
2: 1-4, 14,	The vision is for an appointed time.
18-20	The Lord is in His Holy Temple . . .
3: 1-2,	The Lord had described to Habakkuk the calamities that were to come on His people by the Chaldeans, and the punishment that awaited them. Habakkuk beseeched the Lord to hasten the redemption of His people. (Shigionoth means to wander.) In his prayer, Habakkuk wandered through the events of the past (he appeared to be wavering between fear and trust), and how God's power prevailed.
16 -19	The Amplified version of the Bible suggests waiting patiently. Try memorizing 3: 18.

The end of the book of Habakkuk

****

****

Jeremiah (629 - 588 BC)

(Jeremiah's prophesies came after the fall of Samaria and are spoken to Judah/Jerusalem and families of the house of Israel that were still there. Israel could mean the nation that sprang from Jacob or the land in which they dwelt.

Jeremiah found his ministry difficult at times because he was required by the Lord to pronounce judgment upon the people he loved. He warned God's people of the catastrophe that would come because of rebellion and idol worship; Jeremiah was imprisoned several times because of his words. He lived to see some of his prophesies fulfilled: the fall of Jerusalem to king Nebuchadnezzar/Nebuchadrezzar of Babylon, the destruction of Jerusalem and the Temple, as well as the carrying away of Judah's king and many of the people. The chapters in this book are not all in chronological order.

One might wonder why the same messages were prophesied over and over throughout this book. It was written over a period of about 40 years, and the people of God would hear the message from the Lord but not obey.

God's people were deceived by the surrounding nations and continued to fall into idol worship, even after the foretelling of their coming captivity. The Lord kept crying out through Jeremiah, as well as other prophets, for His people to come back to Him the only true Almighty God. He was reminding them of His mighty miracles performed during their fathers' deliverance from Egyptian bondage. They were captured, carried away to Babylon, and the city of Jerusalem was destroyed. He also prophesied of the eventual return of people form exile and restoration of the nation Israel.)

(629 BC)
Jeremiah

1: 1-10	Anathoth was a city North East of Jerusalem. Chapter 1 is Jeremiah's call of God. A child meaning he thought himself too young and not eloquent enough to speak God's Words.
1: 14-19	Evil from the North - The Lord was speaking encouragement to Jeremiah regarding his assignment.

Jeremiah

2: 4-8, 13,	God is reminding them of a time when they served Him. Then, a cry to Jerusalem, all Judah, and Israel. God then asked what their fathers found in Him that turned them away. (Broken cistern means an empty way of thinking.)
16-17,	These are two Egyptian cities, also known as Memphis and Daphne. Judah's king had been slain in battle with Egypt, thus the crown of Judah's head was broken. They brought the trouble upon themselves in verses 19- 23.
26-32,	Here the Lord is speaking to Judah regarding Israel's idol worship and their trouble.

2: 35-37	They were crying out to God, without repentance, claiming to be innocent. Hands on head was their mode of expressing great grief, and that someone is experiencing the heavy hand of God's affliction.

****

(629 BC)
Jeremiah

3: 4-5,	In verses 1- 3, the Lord is saying the land is polluted because of the sin of unfaithfulness to Him - comparing them to an unfaithful wife and Himself as the husband. He goes on to condemn their wickedness, and their refusal to be ashamed. Will He be angry forever? . . . Verses 7-10 refer to Judah as Israel's sister who saw Israel's sins but feared not the Lord. Judah also sinned against Him.
11-13,	God's appeal and his mercy - Under every green tree they had worshipped strangers/idols.
15-19	The day shall come. They shall look no more to the Ark of the Covenant to seek God; they will have a relationship with Him comparable to a wonderful Father, and not turn away from Him again. Verses 20 - 25 continue in an allegory regarding their backsliding like a wife departing from her husband. The Lord's response is in chapter 4.

(612 BC)
Jeremiah

4: 1-3	(Not remove means not waver or turn away again.) Verses 4-13 continue in expressive language of that era with His exhortation for them to repent. Verses 14 - 31 are Jeremiah's warning that affliction is on the way, and destruction is coming.
5: 1-2, 9,	Verses 1 - 14 are about Jerusalem, and looking for someone who seeks truth. The Lord said they have all forsaken Me. The prophet's figures of speech continue regarding the Lord's punishment.

14-15,	The Lord's Word in Jeremiah's mouth will be like a fire when spoken. A mighty nation will come against them; they will serve strangers in a land that is not theirs - continuing through verse 21.
22-25,	The Lord was asking if they have no fear of Him.
30-31	An appalling and horrible thing . . .

6: 1, 8-9, 13-23,	This is judgment against Jerusalem. Evil is on the way. Tekoa was a city twelve miles south of Jerusalem, near the town of Bethhaccerem in Judah. Zion, is the southwest hill of Jerusalem, also called the city of David. At times, the daughter of Zion could figuratively refer to Jerusalem, or servant of the Lord.
30	The Lord will reject those who refuse to repent. Reprobate here means refused or rejected.

****

(600 BC)
Jeremiah

7: 1-16,	Repent and I will . . . Their sins . . . Shiloh was a city in Ephraim, the first seat of the tabernacle/House of God until the time of
20-30	Samuel. (See I Samuel 4.) Verses 17-19 tell of their worship to an idol named the queen of heaven and to other idols. Then comes a call to repent, and ends describing God's judgment.

8: 1-7,	Here we see the justice of God allowing punishment by the
9-13, 18	Babylonians on those who remain. Jeremiah was to ask God's people why they continue to backslide, and refuse to repent. The priests and prophets had rejected the Word of the Lord, and dealt falsely saying there was peace when no peace came. They shall be overthrown. The Lord continued to speak through Jeremiah that war horses are on the way (verse 16). The chapter ends with Jeremiah lamenting for his people. (Black in verse 21 means in mourning.)

(600 BC)
Jeremiah

9: 1-6,	Next we can see the Lord lamenting for His people; then more about the evil behaviors. (Wormwood - harsh or embittering; gall/*rosh* - a
13-17,	poisonous herb; mourning women - hired professional mourners whose hair was disheveled, their clothes torn, and their countenances daubed with paint and dirt. Their singing would be mingled with shrill
23-24	screams and loud wailing . . . to the noise of tambourines - verses 17-22).

****

10: 1-13,	Idols born - meaning carried. There is none like the Lord. God's Judgment of their sins and His greatness continue through 14 - 21.
22	This refers to the coming of the invading Chaldean army. (Bruit here means hearing or report.) In 23-25, Jeremiah is asking the Lord for correction, but not to be too harsh.

(608 BC)
Jeremiah

11: 1-14,	This is a warning to Judah and Jerusalem against disobedience, because
17	they have turned away to serve idols. The end of chapter 11 is a plot against Jeremiah's life.

****

12: 1-2,	The ancient meaning of reigns is desire of the heart. Jeremiah asked God how long the wicked would prosper. Verses 3 - 13 are graphic details.
14-17	The Lord is speaking to Judah's wicked neighbors who are not sincere - if . . .

13: 19, 24-25	Judah shall be carried away captive. Verses 1-18 are an allegory in which the Lord exhorted His people to repent.
14: 1,	A dearth/drought continues through verse 9. This has a spiritual
10-15,	meaning as well; they feel like the Lord has forsaken them, then
20-22	they pray.

| 15: 1, 4-6,
14-17 | God is telling Jeremiah that even if Moses and Samuel requested Him to change His mind, He would not; they will be removed to a strange land. (See II Kings: 21: 11-12.) |

(Hezekiah was the king of Judah that did not accept the Prophet Isaiah's Word from God that he was going to die. He cried out to God and was granted 15 more years. Manasseh, his son, was born of that 15 added years and he became the most wicked king of Judah. This in recorded in II Kings 21.)

Jeremiah

| 15: 20-21, | Jeremiah cried out to the Lord regarding himself, and his faithfulness in his prophetic ministry. God answered Jeremiah in that He will take care of the Israelites who have fought against him for speaking God's Word, also God will give him favor. That promise of favor was fulfilled when the people were carried away to Babylon. Jeremiah was treated well according to the commands of Nebuchadnezzar king of Babylon. (See Jere.39:11-12). |

****

| 16: 10-15,
19, 21 | The Lord is speaking to Israel through the prophet; God is taking His peace, loving-kindness, and mercies away from His rebellious people. Again we read about the exile, and their eventual return. |

| 17: 7-8, 9 | The message is about sin and punishment in 1 - 6, then the blessed person... See Psalm 1.
Verse 9 tells what man's heart is like without the Lord. This chapter continues with the importance of observing the Sabbath. |

Jeremiah

| 18: 1-12,
18 | He (God) is the potter, we are the clay. Verses 18-23 are a plot against Jeremiah for speaking God's judgments. |

This book continues through chapter 25 with threatened judgment, complaints of Jeremiah, captivity foretold, false prophets, and nations destroyed. The 70 years of captivity is foretold in 25: 11.

19: 2, 15	The Lord was referring to Jerusalem as the valley of Hinnom. Hinnom/ Tophet was a place of horrible inhuman sacrifices which caused its name to be detested. We can read that Josiah abolished worship of the idol Molech there in II Kings 23:10.
20: 1-3, 9, 11	Jeremiah's persecution (Magormissabib means terror is round about.)- In spite of being persecuted, he continued speaking the Words of the Lord for God's Words were like a burning fire shut up in his bones.

(589 BC)
Jeremiah

21: 1-10, 14	In chapter 21, the people of Jerusalem are urged to submit to the king of Babylon because they are being punished for their sins; God Himself will be fighting against them. Those who don't go to Babylon will die.

****

(609 BC)

22: 1-9, 25	God instructed Jeremiah to go to the king's house and speak God's Word - judgment on the wicked and blessings for the obedient. The chapter continues with more about the judgment to come.
23: 1-4, **5-6**, 7-14, 21-22, 29-32	Here is judgment against the pastors who have driven God's people away from Him, and foretelling of the Messiah whom we know is Jesus. Verse 9 tells of Jeremiah's grief about all the Lord is saying. The chapter continues with more about wicked prophets.

(598 BC)

24: 1-10	The beginning of chapter 24 is a parable of figs and ends with the interpretation.

****

(606 BC)

25: 1-13, 31	The Word of the Lord to Judah - a prophesy regarding the 70 years of Babylonian captivity. Then Babylon will be punished; the chapter continues foretelling vividly the ruin of the nations.

(Hissing is an expression of contempt, also take note of the dating for some of the chapters in Jeremiah.)

(609 BC)

26: 1-17,   *(Details about Shiloh are in I Samuel chapter 4.)* The people came against Jeremiah. Chapter 26 continues with the elder's discourse

24   regarding previous prophets.

27:1-2, 22   This begins with a parable regarding submission to Babylon, and may be read in its entirety by all. The nations are to serve Nebuchadnezzar, (v. 9-11, v. 12-15), for an appointed time, and in verse 22 there is a repeat of the promise that Israel would return to their land.

28: 15-17   Hananiah stood up in the house of the Lord and declared a false prophesy. The Word of the Lord came to Jeremiah, starting in verse 12, instructing him to speak God's Word to Hananiah. God's Word included the death of that false prophet for speaking lies to the people.

****

(599 BC)

Jeremiah

29: 1-32,   Jeremiah sent a letter to those who were taken to Babylon from Jerusalem. Seek peace in the city of captivity, and seek the Lord with all your heart. (Jeremiah 29: 11-13 & 33: 3 are good memory verses.) They had struggles because of the false prophets; the chapter continues with details of false prophets the Lord will punish.

****

(606 BC)

Jeremiah

30: 1-3, 18,   Write My Words down in a book. The Lord promised that Israel and

20,   Judah will return to their own land, and their enemies will be punished.

22-24   This promise continues in 31: 1.

(Even though the dates for all these chapters are not in order, all this foretelling of the captivity, and return was years before those events took place. The captivity process started with besiege against Israel about 721 BC; it was completed about 586 BC with the destruction of Jerusalem. Rebuilding of the temple was completed in 515 BC.)

31: 1, 10-14,	
24-25,	Restoration was promised. This chapter continues with encouragement.
31-34	A New Covenant is promised which will be a new way of life under the Messiah, Jesus. We know He came, and He is coming a second time. Old Testament believers had no understanding of the two comings.

****

(590 BC)

32: 1-5,	The Word of the Lord came again to Jeremiah remembering how God had brought their fathers out of Egypt, and how they had rebelled
17-34,	and sinned against God. Their current sins and captivity is
36-42	discussed here as well as God's great power, and the glorious return to their own land.

****

Jeremiah
(590 BC)

33: 1-3, 7-9,	Jeremiah was in prison. Cleansing God's people from iniquity was promised.
12-22	In that day . . . the Branch of Righteousness is our Savior Jesus, the Messiah. As surely as day and night come, God's covenant is sure. His promise continues to the end of the chapter. **(33: 15-16)**

(591 BC)

34: 1-3	This prophesy regarding Jerusalem is before the exile to Babylon. The ruin of Jerusalem is foretold.
21-22	The people in Jerusalem broke their covenant to set servants free after 7 years of service. The chapter ends with God's response.

(607 BC)
Jeremiah

35: 16-19   Chapter 35 gives details regarding the Rechabites (descendants of Rechab) obeying the commands of their father Jonadab. This is contrasted with the rebellion and disobedience of Jerusalem and Judea. God's response . . .

36: 1-4, 10,   Baruch the scribe wrote Jeremiah's words in a scroll. He read what he had written in the chamber of Gemariah the son of Shaphan (the secretary to King Josiah) in the House of the Lord.

    21-23,   The king had the scroll burned.

    27-32   Jeremiah's words were written again.

****

37: 3-21   King Zedekiah requested Jeremiah to pray and get a Word from the Lord. Egypt will not save Judah from the Chaldeans. Jeremiah was accused of deserting to the Chaldeans; he was cast into prison. Jeremiah's time of imprisonment continues in chapter 38.

38: 2-21,   This chapter begins with the foul treatment of Jeremiah for proclaiming

    28   God's Word, then King Zedekiah speaks with Jeremiah.

(590 BC)

39: 1-2,   Jerusalem was besieged. About 1 1/2 years later the city was broken into. Verses 4-6 tell what the king of Babylon did to

    8-12,   King Zedekiah of Judah, then information about the people who were still in the city. Jeremiah's fate . . .

    14-18   Ebedmelech was the man responsible for getting Jeremiah out of the cistern/pit (Jere. 38: 7-13). *(Prey means reward of battle.)*

****

(588 BC)
Jeremiah

40: 1-6,   Jeremiah was loosed from prison and was shown favor. In verse 5, he

    11-16   received food and a release from the Babylonian captain of the guard. Jeremiah then went to Gedaliah who had been assigned by the King of

Babylon to be the governor in the land of Judah. He dwelt with Gedaliah in Mizpah, a city of Benjamin four miles northwest of Jerusalem. An Ammonite named Ishmael was sent to slay Gedaliah.

41: 1-8, 10-18	Ishmael continued to slay Jews who had been left in their land and he attempted to take captives. *(Verses 17 & 18 are all one sentence.)*

42: 1-19,	Jeremiah was asked by the people to seek the Lord on their behalf. The Word of the Lord came to Jeremiah. *(Execration in verse 18 means a detested thing or a curse)*

****

(588 BC)
Jeremiah

43: 1- 7	The people disobeyed and went to Egypt taking all the remnant of Judah including Jeremiah. The chapter ends with God's Word to Jeremiah that the Lord will send Nebuchadnezzar aginst Egypt.

44: 1-30	This tells of the Jews who were in Egypt, their deliberate disobedience, that only a small number will escape the sword, and those who escape will return to Judah.

(In order to avoid confusion of event timing, the following information is provided. According to chronological dating the chapters from 36 forward very possibly should be in this order - from earliest to most current starting with 607 BC and ending at 587 BC: Chapter 36, 45, 46, 47, 48, 49, 50, 51, 37, 39, 38, 40, 41, 42, 52, 43, then 44. It is stated in chapters 36: 1 & 45: 1 that King Jehoiakim was king of Judah, and in chapter 39: 1 Zedekiah, the last king of Judah, reigned. See Kings chart in appendix.)

(607 BC)

45: 1-5	To Baruch the scribe -
46: 1-2, 8, 13-14, 20,	The Word of the Lord against Egypt . . .
27-28	God is encouraging Judah and Israel.

****

(600 BC)

47: 1	This chapter is a prophesy against the Philistines.
48: 1, 7-8, 16	Next is a warning against Moab: Nebo was a god of Babylon, Kiriathaim/a town in Moab, and Misgab/Mizpeh a city of Moab. Chemosh was the national god of the Moabites and Ammonites; Moloch may have been the same god. Judgment on Moab continues throughout chapter 48.

Jeremiah

49: 1-2, 6, 17-18, 27,	Chapter 49 begins with Judgment of the Ammonites. Later the Ammonites took over the area of the tribe of Gad's inheritance (after the captivity). *(Daughters is referring to villages.)* Rabbah was the capital city that was to be burned down, but the Lord said Ammon will prosper again. Verse 7 begins a prophesy against Edom. In 23 it turns to Damascus, then Kedar, and Hazor.
38-39	Verses 34-39 are the Lord's judgment against Elam - a district south of Assyria. In the latter days it will be restored.

(595 BC)

50: 1-3, 4-10, 13-15, 17-20, 29-31, 39-40, 46	Judgment continues, now against Babylon. Bel was the national god of the Babylonians and Merodach an image they worshipped. In that time, Israel and Judah will be seeking the Lord; the Chaldeans and Babylon will be overtaken. God's redemption of Israel . . . Mount Carmel and the Land of Bashan . . .

****

(595 BC)

Jeremiah

51: 1, 5, 10,	Jeremiah continues to prophesy against Babylon, then against Israel and Judah.
15-16, 24, 29,	Next he speaks of the Greatness of God, then warnings to Babylon and all Chaldea.
43-44,	As mentioned earlier, Bel was the national god of the Babylonians.

60-64　　Jeremiah wrote it all in a book. Seraiah is his messenger. Chapter 52 is not a prophesy; what it records had already happened. Jeremiah lived to see some of his prophesies come to pass. Zedekiah was the last king of Judah reigning in Jerusalem. The destruction of Jerusalem and captivity were at the end of his reign.

(588 BC)
Jeremiah
52: 4-5,　　At this time, the House of the Lord and other houses were burned, the
　12-23,　　walls of Jerusalem broken down, people as well as valuable items from the House of the Lord were carried away.

31-34　　This book closes with favor to Jehoiachin by the new king of Babylon.

The end of the book of Jeremiah
****

****

Nebuchadnezzar again besieged Jerusalem and Jehoiachin surrendered. At that time, all but the poorest were carried away. See II Kings 24: 8-16. They were taken to Telabib and other towns along the Chebar River nearly 200 miles north of Babylon.

(In war against Assyria, Pharaoh-Necho killed King Josiah of Judah, who was the father of Eliakim. Pharaoh-Necho changed Eliakim's name to Jehoiakim. Jehoiakim was the father of Jehoiachin.)

Ezekiel was also taken away to Mesopotamia by Nebuchadnezzar with Jehoiachin/Jeconiah King of Judah, and 3,000 people. Ezekiel was in captivity when he received the prophesies from the Lord and was kept there until the fourteenth year after the destruction of Jerusalem. Ezekiel's purpose was to comfort the captives.

(595 - 574 BC)
Ezekiel
1: 1-28　　The Word of the Lord came to Ezekiel in a vision. This continues with the description of the 4 living creatures from verse 6 - 21.
　　　　　　A voice . . . He saw the Throne and the Glory of the Lord.

	(A memory challenge is 1: 26-28.)
2: 1-7	Chapter 2 is a continuation of chapter 1.
	Verse 6 through 3: 3 is the Lord giving Ezekiel His Words to speak.
3: 4-5, 7,	
10-11, 17,	*(In verse 9 adamant means stone, and in verse 14 bitterness is difficulty.)*
	Verses 18-27 are the Lord's instruction to Ezekiel; in 18 the Lord told
22-23	Ezekiel He will hold him accountable. Chapter 4 is the Lord commanding Ezekiel to put together a symbolic siege representing the Chaldean siege on Jerusalem. Directions continue for what he is to do.

(594 BC)

Ezekiel

5: 5- 8,	Verses 1-5 is Ezekiel's directions in symbolic language. Then the
11, 13	prophet speaks to Jerusalem regarding God's judgment on them for their wickedness.
	He continues speaking to the people of Jerusalem.

6: 1-4, 11,	Judgment on Israel . . . *(Diblath which is also Riblah was the site of*
14	*detestable acts of Nebuchadnezzar against Zedekiah (II Kings 25: 7) and Pharaoh Necho against Jehoahaz (II Chron. 36).*

****

7: 1-4, 8-9,	Judgment on Israel continues.
16, 22,	They will profane the Temple.
25 -27	
8: 1-18	This is the vision of the Glory of the Lord which is also in Chapter 1. In verse 5, the vision of the Temple continued and Ezekiel was shown all the abominations the people of Judah were doing in the Temple of the Lord. *(Image of jealousy/semel means idol and Jaazaniah was the leader of the seventy elders worshiping idols. Branch to the nose was a means of superstitious worship; the worshippers held a branch before their mouth.)*

Ezekiel	The revelation continues in chapters 9 - 11; Ezekiel could see which

9: 8-10	persons were grieving because of the abominations. Then he saw the rest of the people slain. The Lord was showing that He knows who has been faithful to Him; they will be saved.
	The Lord explains that the people who were to be destroyed had brought it upon themselves because of their wickedness.
10: 1-22	This is the cherubims at the House of the Lord.

****

11: 1-2,	He also saw those who caused the wickedness.
4-12,	They will be delivered to strangers, and taken away from Jerusalem to be punished. *(Caldron means pot. The city was like a cooking pot filled with the slain.)*
16-21,	These verses are a promise of salvation; God's people will be gathered and return to Israel. The wicked . . .
22-25	When the vision disappeared, Ezekiel spoke the Word of the Lord to the captives where he and they resided in Chaldea.

(594 BC)
Ezekiel

12: 10,	Verses 1-16 are a picturesque rendering of what was about to happen
15-16,	to the prince in Jerusalem, and those who were still there. A few shall remain and confess Israel's detestable abominations to the people in surrounding nations, thus they will understand the justice of the Lord.
20, 25-28	God's Word will come to pass!
13: 1, 6-8,	To the false prophets . . . Verses 10 - 16 are a symbolic description of what will happen to the false prophets. He describes a wall that was not built properly, then whitewashed to make it look good.
17,	This is to female false prophets with more dramatic descriptions through verses 18-21.
22-23	Their false visions and divination practices will stop.

****

14: 1-4,	These verses tell of self will and idols of silver and gold.

14: 6-8,	The Lord tells them to repent. Next in 9 - 11, the Lord speaks against idol worshippers who go to God's prophets to inquire of the Lord - He will answer them Himself.
12-14,	Against the people of the land - A person is protected by his own righteousness not that of another. In 15 - 21, this theme continues in graphic language.
22-23	The Lord is comforting Ezekiel in that He does not punish without cause.

(594 BC)
Ezekiel

	Chapter 15: 1-7 is a parable of a vine tree or grapevine - meaning Israel.
15: 8	The land will be desolate.

16: 1-3,	Next is a symbolic description of Israel's beginning; how the Lord took them for His own and blessed them. He spoke through Ezekiel to tell His people they behave more like the accursed Canaanites than Israelites. They partook of the behaviors of the Amorites and Hittites who were the most corrupt Canaanites.

This narrative continues with their prideful behavior, how they turned away from Him to serve false gods in idol worship, and other detestable practices.

God spoke to Ezekiel in verses 6-14 regarding how He forgave them, and blessed them. Starting in verse 15, they continued in the abominable practices of the heathens. *(The language and figurative speech were in conformity to those times and places.)*

Ezekiel

16: 60 - 63	This chapter continues with graphic metaphors about their abominations, and then closes with God's plan for His mercy and forgiveness - a New Covenant.

Chapter 17 is a parable of two eagles and a vine. It speaks of Israel looking to Egypt for help instead of seeking God, then the exile to Babylon.

18: 20, 30	Chapter 18 in a parable of sour grapes: Obey God and you shall live - children will not be guilty for the iniquity of their father - repent.

****

19: 1	A lamentation for the princes of Israel continues through this chapter in another parable.
(593 BC)	
20: 1-13,	God would not speak directly to the elders of Israel; He spoke through His prophet Ezekiel. Then in 15 - 26, is a remembrance of their deliverance from Egypt, and 40 years in the wilderness because of their sins.
28-29,	Bamah means any place of idolatrous worship.
33-34,	
40-48	Toward the South meaning Judah and Jerusalem as they are South of Mesopotamia where the prophet then dwelt as a captive.

****

Ezekiel	
21: 1-2,	Here is a warning against Jerusalem and all Israel. This chapter is a parable about swords. Verses 3-17 tell of the Lord's sword. In 18-24 the prophet speaks of Babylon's sword, their king's divinations regarding the Ammonites, and Jerusalem.
25, 31	Israel . . . Next, the sword is coming against the Ammonites.
22: 1, 4, 8,	Thy time has come . . .
12-15,	(usury - high interest charged) They will be scattered. God refining
22,	Israel as silver in a furnace is in verses 17-22.
26-27, 30-31	
(593 BC)	
Ezekiel	Chapter 23 is the Word of the Lord against Samaria and Jerusalem in
23: 23-24,	graphic descriptions of their sins.
28, 38	
(590 BC)	
Ezekiel	
24: 1-2,	Verses 1-13 is a parable of a pot on the fire boiling bones of a choice animal.

24: 14,	This is judgment that will come to pass. After the destruction of the temple and some of the people were gone into exile, Ezekiel was to be a
27	sign to those who remained.

****

25: 1-7,	The Word of the Lord against the Ammonites - *(1 - Aha is a word used to express surprise and pleasure. 2. Rabbah was the chief city of the Ammonites and was east of Jordan. 3 - Couching place refers to a fold or place to keep their flocks and 4 - despite is spite or malice which is a desire to harm others.)*
25: 10-17	Judgment continues against Ammon and Moab. See a Bible map of Moab, Ammon, and Edom. *(Teman was a district in the northeast part of Edom and Dedan was a district near Edom. The Philistine area was west of Jerusalem by the Mediterranean Sea and the Cherethims, of Philistine origin, were descendants of King David's body guards.)*
(588 BC) Ezekiel	
26: 1-7, 13,	This is the Lord revealing to Ezekiel what the people of Tyrus are saying; they are cheering because Jerusalem has fallen. *(Tyrus/Tyre*
16-19,	*was a very wealthy city in the center of Phoenicia on the coast of the*
21	*Mediterranean Sea. The Israelites did not drive the Canaanites out of Tyre and Sidon and other Phoenician cities as Moses had commanded. They were friendly for a period of time.)*
	The Lord's answer: He will bring many nations against Tyrus and King Nebuchadnezzar (same as Nebuchadrezzar) of Babylon, and will attack with a huge army. This continues in expressive language. The kings of the nations around them will tremble in fear at what is happening to this famous city, and to her ships on the sea.

****

27: 1,	This chapter is a continuation of 26. The Lord is speaking against the boasting that had come from Tyrus. They were situated on the sea in a perfect place for commerce with other areas.
10-11,	Soldiers from other places served in their army and made Tyrus great.
12-25,	They traded with cities on the Mediterranean as far as Greece and

27: 34-36	Spain. On land they traded to the Tigris and cities south. In the time of the fall and destruction, like a ship at sea loaded with cargo, all will be lost when the ship sinks.
28: 6-10,	This is still judgment on Tyrus. Verses 1- 5 are a reproof to the ruler of Tyrus for being so proud that he believed himself to be God. Verses 11-19 continues in irony telling him he has polluted his Eden, defiled his sanctuaries, and he is expelled from his paradise. (This speaks of the fall of Satan which was also in a prophesy against
20-22, 25-26	the King of Babylon in Isaiah 14). This chapter ends with a prophesy against Zidon, and a promise to Israel.

****

(589 BC)
Ezekiel

29: 1-3, 9,	Judgment is coming against Egypt. Again the Lord is dealing with pride, this time in Pharaoh. Pathros is a district in Egypt. Base
13-16	kingdom means humble. Israel will not rely on Egypt any more. In 17-21 we see God's wages to the king of Babylon for his army accomplishing God's purpose over Tyrus and Egypt.

(572 BC)

30: 3,	The day is near that the prior prophesies will come to pass. This
13, 19	chapter describes the desolation; the king of Babylon will come against Egypt, and they will be scattered.

(588 BC)
Ezekiel

31: 1	This is a parable about Assyria being recompensed for her pride, then in verse 18, the Lord says the same will happen to Egypt.

(587 BC)

32: 1, 11, 15, 32	This is a graphic description of the King of Babylon coming against Egypt. Pharaoh laid (died) in the midst of the heathens.

33: 7-11, 21,	Ezekiel was chosen of the Lord to be a watchman for Israel. He will hear from the Lord and then go and speak God's Word to Israel. Verses 11-20 speaks of righteous and unrighteous; turn from your unrighteousness and don't go back to your sinful ways.

33: 29-33	The people listen to Ezekiel but do not obey.

34: 12,	The shepherds (rulers) are not providing what the flock (people) needs. They take care of themselves but never tend the sheep. Thus, the sheep wandered. The Lord will remove the leaders and rescue the sheep.
23-24,	Prophesy of the shepherd to come - (Jesus came).
27, 30-31	

****

Ezekiel

35: 1-5,	Judgment of Mount Seir (in Edom) at the time of the Babylonian
9-14	conquest. . . Edom pridefully proclaimed they will possess Israel and Judah even though the Lord is there.

36: 1, 6-11,	This prophesy is a personification addressed to the mountains of Israel. The Edomites/Idumea took possession of the mountains of Israel after the Babylonian captivity. The mountains will be freed from their foes and the dishonor of their idols. (Idol worship by the Jews was the cause of their dispersion and captivity.)
19-24,	Israel will return, and they will be more prosperous than ever.
25-28,	The New Covenant. . .
33-38	In that day . . .

****

Ezekiel

37: 11-14,	This chapter is a parable of dry bones in a vision along with the interpretation.
22-28	The dry bones represented the hopeless state of the dispersed Jews. God will restore the people from captivity into the land of their forefathers as one nation. There is a transition in the vision to the time of the Gospel dispensation, and Christianity, as well as the eternal promise. They will no longer be under heathen rulers, but be in one nation as one flock with one Shepherd.

38: 1-3,	To begin this explanation, here is a quote from Adam Clark's Commentary: *"This* (referring to chapters 38 & 39) *could be the most difficult prophesy in the Old Testament. It's difficult to know the king or people intended."* However, it may not be quite that difficult! Gog, as used by Ezekiel means the chief or head of Magog. Magog here being the nation/area North of Syria along the Mediterranean Sea, Greece, Asia Minor, Asia, and Europe. Syria could be alluding to Antiochus Epiphanes' artful and cunning ways. (You may want to check the note in the Amplified Bible regarding Gog in verse 1.)
	Tubal and Meshech were sons of Japheth who was the son of Noah. The North nations would have been areas populated by their tribes. Verse 2 appears to be a prophesy against the Northern nations who were great enemies of Israel. Verses 4-7 tell that those people of the North will come against Israel with a mighty army, but they will not prevail/win.
Ezekiel 38: 8,	The people of Israel will be brought back to their land, and will dwell securely.
10-12, 14-16,	Evil plans would be devised against Israel and a mighty army will come against her; however, Israel's opposing armies will be destroyed in the latter days, by the Lord.
19,	In that day . . . the earth shall tremble and shake at the Presence of the Lord.
23	In verse 22 the Lord will plead/judge against Israel's opposing armies, and He will be magnified.

****

(587 BC)
Ezekiel

39: 1, 7,	Chapter 39 continues with the same theme. In verses 11 - 12, Hamongog means multitude of Gog. The multitudes of Gog will be buried, and it will take 7 months to bury them. The name of the city
16,	where the burying is to take place shall be Hamonah.

39: 25-29	The restoration in chapters 38 & 39 appear to be the latter days/end times, which includes spiritual Israel/Christians.
(574 BC) Ezekiel 40: 1,	This vision of the new temple was to be declared to Israel. It is the measurements of the outer and inner courts, posts, tables whereon to slay sacrifices, size of the building, porch, gates, chambers, windows, roof, etc.
46	The sons of Levi . . .
	Chapter 41 and 42 are a continuation with details of the measurements and directions. Chapter 42 is measurements of the chambers and outside walls.
42: 20	A wall is to separate the Sanctuary (the holy temple proper) from the profane (common outer area).

****

43: 1-7, 10-12	God's Glory will return to the temple. See Chapter 1: 4, 26-28 and 10: 4. Verses 13-27 are information that is to be proclaimed to the people regarding altar measurements, offerings, and the temple.
44: 1	Information about the Sanctuary, and duties of the Levites continue throughout this chapter.
(574 BC) Ezekiel 45: 1-8	These verses tell of the division of the land for the Sanctuary, the Levites (ministers in the House of the Lord), the prince (leader or exalted one), and the tribes. Offering information is in verses 9-25.
46: 1-3	Offerings . . .
18 -20	The chapter continues through verse 24 regarding the inheritance of the prince and the offering place.
47: 1-9,	Ezekiel's vision of the holy waters - (Verse 2, he meaning the one in 40: 3-4, . . . all that I shall show thee). Analogy: v. 1 Under the threshold - humility, God resists the proud.

v.2 North was Dan - Dan means responsibility and discipline.

v.2 East was Judah - praise.

v.3 Through the waters - walking in the Spirit with positive obedience.

v.4 To the knees - doing business with God in prayer. To the loins - strong, receiving strength from God.

v. 5 To swim - dependent on God; go in over your head and trust God.

v. 8 Healing waters - healing of everything.

v. 9 We are to be fishers of men out in the deep.

12, 21 (574 BC) Ezekiel	These verses are about the borders of each tribe's possession. The book ends with chapter 48 describing what portions of land the tribes are to receive.

The end of the book of Ezekiel

****

****

(According to the dates, Obadiah and Lamentations would come between Ezekiel 39 & 40.)

Esau, the one who sold his birthright, is Edom. His name was changed in Genesis 25. Obadiah's prophesy is referring to the descendants of Edom. The ancient name of Edom was Mt. Seir; Esau drove out the Horites/Horims and changed the name to Edom. (Deut. 2: 12; Gen. 14: 6)

(587 BC)
Obadiah

1: 3 -4, 8-10, 12-13, 15, 17, 21	Edom rejoiced when Judah was taken captive. Teman was in the southern area of Edom. This is a promise to Judah, Jacob's descendants, then the Lord's judgment…

The end of the book of Obadiah

****

Lamentations

Lamentations is the prophet Jeremiah lamenting, in poetic language, the destruction of Jerusalem in 586 BC, as well as the ruin and exile that followed. His prayer and a note of trust are included.

(586 BC)

Lamentations

1: 1, 5, 16	In verse 1, become tributary means fallen into slavery.
2: 1-2, 11	Chapter 2 is an expressive description of the Lord's destruction of Jerusalem; He is allowing them to be overtaken by their enemy. (daughter/descendants - Zion/Jerusalem) The prophet's distress is revealed in verses 11 - 22.
3: 1-2, 21-27	He is bewailing severe trials of his own life in verses 1-20. Darkness refers to calamities and light to prosperity. In 21 - 66 he recalls the Lord's mercy and calls out to Him.
4: 1-2, 12-13	There is a contrast here between current devastation and former prosperity. The chapter continues with lamenting the calamities in 17 - 20 and a promise of deliverance in verse 22.
5: 9-21	They are crying out to God in repentance and hope of deliverance. (The prayer was answered 70 years later when the Israelites were set free from their bondage in Babylon. They were allowed to return to their own land.)

The end of the book of Lamentations

****

****

Daniel (607-534 BC)

(Please note that neither the captivity and carrying away of the Jews, nor the restoration was a quick activity. Israel and Judah were besieged for many years before their captivity. Israel, as stated in another place in this study, was conquered and carried away before Judah and Jerusalem. The Medo Persian king, Cyrus, conquered Babylon and made the proclamation for the Jews to return to their homeland. Darius was given charge over Babylonia. This is covered in more detail after chapter 5.

Another notation that is important is the dating of the chapters in Daniel. As with all the dates, they may not be exact but they are in a more chronological order to better understand the events. The study has some of the chapters moved from the usual order for that purpose.)

1: 1-21   Jerusalem was besieged; some vessels from the House of the Lord, and certain youths were taken away. *(They were not little ones. In the original language, ben, means sons not children as recorded in KJV; see the description of them in verse 4, and three years later in verse 20. Definitions in verses 10 to 15 are as follows: sort/age; pulse/beans; meat/food; and fatter/better looking.)* Verse 7 gives their names. Daniel's new name was Belteshazzar not to be confused with Nebuchadnezzar's son Belshazzar. Notice their commitment and reliance on Almighty God as you read this book

****

(603 BC)

2: 1-13,   Nebuchadnezzar's dream - (The Chaldeans were one of many tribes in Babylon. They were magicians, astronomers, and priests who were idol worshipers interested in learning and science.)

   14-30,   Daniel sought God to receive interpretation of the king's dream.

   31-49   This vision may be interpreted as follows:
            gold - Babylon, silver - Medo Persian, brass - Greek (Alexander the Great), iron - Roman, iron and clay - Roman and other barbarian nations. The stone is Jesus' kingdom.

****

(580 BC)
Daniel

3: 1-18,   Chapter 3 records information about Chaldean idol worship and the gold image. These Jewish men refused to compromise their beliefs in Almighty God, and did not even consider the consequences. They depended completely on God.

3: 19-30	The fiery furnace, God's deliverance, and Nebuchadnezzar's response -

****

(570 BC)
Daniel

4: 1-27,	Chapter 4 tells of the second dream and Daniel's interpretation.

****

28-37	In spite of Nebuchadnezzar's pride, he finally acknowledged God. (*Daniel 5 and 6 are after chapter 8.*)

****

(555 BC)
Daniel   *(Belshazzar was the son of Nebuchadnezzar. At times father is used in Scripture for descendants.)*

7: 1-8,	An interpretation of Daniel's dream - First the lion- Babylon, then the bear - Persia, next the leopard - the Grecian empire, and the fourth represents the Roman empire. Verse 8 refers to the antichrist who will come in the final end times.
9-12,	The Ancient of Days is Almighty God.
7: 13-14,	In a vision, Daniel saw Jesus, Father God, and Jesus' eternal kingdom.
15-28	In the end, Almighty God will have His way; Jesus will reign over the kingdom of the saints of God - those who believe in Jesus.

****

(553 BC)
Daniel   Daniel's second vision is recorded in 8: 1-16.

8: 17-19,	Gabriel explained the vision.
23-24,	A deceitful king shall arise with mighty power, but not from himself (power from Satan).
25-27	With a prideful heart he will be destructive, and even stand up against Jesus, who will have returned in those last days. The fierce king will be destroyed without being touched. *Note: He will be destroyed by the power in Jesus' Words - think about that - remember He created the whole world -*

He spoke all things into existence; see Genesis 1 and John 1. Throughout the scriptures we can see that Almighty God used individuals, prophets that He chose, to speak His Words. His Words spoken through the prophets have either already come to pass, or will come to pass at the time they are referring to - end of the age.

****

(538 BC)

Daniel

5: 1-16,	King Belshazzar's feast - (He was the last Babylonian king before Babylonia was conquered by the Medo Persian Empire, and was the son of Nebuchadnezzar, verse 18). He used the vessels from the House of God to worship idols. Then, God's writing on the wall. . .
18-31	This is Daniel's interpretation, the king's pride, and the consequences.

****

Note: This study does not focus on the Medo-Persian Empire; however, some information regarding the Medes and Persians can be helpful in understanding the Scriptures relating to Darius and Cyrus in Isaiah, Jeremiah, Ezra, Nehemiah, Daniel, and Esther, as well as Haggai, Zechariah, and Malachi. There were two rulers named Darius and two with the name of Cyrus during that era of history. One Cyrus was Cyrus the Great also known as Cyrus II.

The Persian King Cyrus II conquered Media in 549 BC. This Kingdom was then referred to as the Medo-Persian Empire and the combination became a very powerful force in the Middle East at that time. Cyrus II was the absolute head of this empire and they conquered Babylon in 539 BC; the restoration of Israel began about 538 BC. (One source referred to Cyrus II as the supreme monarch; however, that kind of title would better be reserved for the King of Kings our Lord and Savior, Jesus Christ.)

Darius the Mede was appointed king/governor (King in the original language - melek - can mean prince, king, or counsellor) over Babylon in 539 BC under King Cyrus the main monarch of the entire Medo-Persian Empire. That was the first year of the reign of King Cyrus of the Medo-Persian Empire over Babylonia as part of his kingdom; he gave the decree for the Jews to return to Jerusalem and rebuild the temple (Ezra chapter 1). The temple was not completed until some years later, about 515 BC. Ezra, in chapter 4, gives the reasons for this. (Additional study could be performed regarding these empires; however, that would be a history study and not part of this Bible study.)

****

(538 BC)

Daniel

6: 1-3,	Darius was King over Babylon. Daniel had favor with the king and Darius set Daniel over Babylon. (Live forever was a greeting at that time to address a king.)

Daniel

6: 4-23	Daniel knew about the king's decree, verse 10, but prayed as usual to Almighty God. He could have prayed privately and no one would have known; however, he chose to leave his windows open and pray in his usual manner. He was totally committed to Almighty God as were the other three Jews first mentioned in chapter 1. Daniel also considered not the consequences; he was honoring God whom he served.
25-28	The consequences - God saved Daniel, then those who tried to trap Daniel were destroyed. King Darius' decree . . . (Verse 28 tells that the reign of Darius was under Persian King Cyrus who was king over all of the Medo-Persian empire.)

****

(538 BC)

9: 1-19	Daniel prayed; he repented on behalf of Israel and Judah.
20- 23, **<u>24-27</u>**	Gabriel arrived; the Most Holy One will return at the appointed time and bring in everlasting righteousness. 9: 24-27 tells of the first coming of Christ and then the appearance of the antichrist. Jesus' second coming will occur during the antichrist's reign. At that time, Jesus will come to destroy not only the antichrist but all evil, and bring in His Everlasting Kingdom. (Weeks referred to years. A week would be 7 years; 70 weeks = 490 years as in Lev. 25: 8.)

****

(534 BC)

Daniel

10: 1-9,   Daniel's prayer and fasting -

  12- 21   He saw Jesus (Rev. 1: 13-15) in a vision who spoke to him about things to come in the last days.

****

(534 BC)

11: 1-4   The vision continues - (*Daniel received visions of events that would come to pass in the Old Testament times as well as Jesus' first and second comings that will bring in His Everlasting Kingdom.*

The kings at that time were: Cyrus; his son, Cambyses; Smerdis who pretended to be another son of Cyrus; Darius, the son of Hystaspes who married the daughter of Cyrus; and Xerxes the son of Darius. A mighty king shall stand up might refer to Alexander the Great who came about 100 years later, and had no sons to reign after him.)

Throughout chapter 11, Daniel speaks of great wickedness and battles between the kings of the northern area (Syria) and the kings of the southern area (Egypt). In the latter part of the chapter, Jerusalem and the Jews as well as Rome are involved in the conflicts. At one point in the vision, the Temple was polluted. The king of the North appeared to win out; however, in verse 45 we can see he shall come to his end. It remains questionable as to the time of all that. Parts have already occurred and documented in history; others could refer to end times especially since the next chapter (12) deals with the taking away of the church and end times.

****

Note: Only the spirit and soul (The soul is our mind, emotions, and will; our spirit is the part of us where the Holy Spirit comes to reside when we receive Jesus as our Lord and Savior.) of believers who die go immediately to be with the Lord. We will receive our glorified bodies and be reunited with our soul and spirit when Jesus returns for believers. (The meaning of sleep is physical death.)

(534 BC)
Daniel

12: 1-4   This will be a time of great trouble and the taking away of the church (we refer to this event as the rapture). See I Thessalonians 4: 13-17; 5: 8-10; II Thess. 1: 7-10; Acts 24: 15; and John 5: 25-29.

12: 5-9,   When will this take place? Trust in the Lord & be ready **(Prov. 3: 5-6)**.
13   Verses 10-13 is more about end times. Adam Clark's commentary states that we are "left totally in the dark" regarding the times here mentioned.

The end of the book of Daniel
****

(588 - 516 BC) This was during the captivity and restoration periods and is a possible time of Psalms 66, 67, 74, 79, 84, 87, 94, 102, 111 - 113, 116, 117, 123, 126, 130, and 137.

****

The Book of Psalms (The Book of Praises)

The Book of Psalms was collected and compiled by Ezra the Scribe after David's death according to *Adam Clarke's Commentary on the Holy Bible.*

David did not write all the psalms; they were <u>composed at different times throughout the Old Testament era</u>. The occasions for some of the writings are pointed out in their contents. Psalms of praise were sung in the Jewish worship services. The Psalms frequently speak of trust and peace as well as other subjects. Psalms may be read at any time not necessarily sandwiched into the chronology of this study.

Psalms 1, 119, and 147 - 150 may have been written in 444 BC.
(These are all suggestions for memorization: Psalm 1: 1-3; 19:14; all of 23; 27: 1, 11, & 14; 29: 11; 34: 1-10; 35: 9; 37: 1-7; 40: 16, 31; 46: 1; 47: 1, 6-7; 81: 1; 91 all; 103: 1-3; 107: 20; 118: 17, 24, 28, 29; 119: 11, 27, 105, 114, 130; 122: 6; 147: 1; 121: 1-8; 136: 1; 45: 3; 147: 1, 5, 11; **2: 2, 7-8; 45: 6-7; 41: 9; 68: 18; and 118: 22, 26.**)

****

Additional information:

- *Babylon was a major power in the world from 612-539 BC.*
- *The destruction of Jerusalem by Nebuchadnezzar's forces was ~586 BC.*
- *Babylonian Captivity period, 586-516 BC.*
- *Nebuchadnezzar finally believed in the Most High God, then he died in 570 BC.*
- *The Fall of Babylon to Persia as the major power was 539 BC with Cyrus as king.*
- *Previously Persia had conquered Media. King Cyrus of Persia began the return of the captive Jews. There was a king Darius who reigned 522 - 485 BC.*

****

(536-457 BC)

Ezra

1: 1-11   This was the fulfillment of a prophesy regarding Cyrus many years before he was born. Isaiah had prophesied this in 712 BC, also see the note between chapters 5 and 6 of Daniel.

Verse 8 - Sheshbozzar is the Babylonian name for Zeruebbel who was a descendent of David (genealogy information).

2:64-65, 70   Chapter 2 lists those who returned from Babylonian captivity. Nethenims means Assistants to the Levites who were descendants of Levi.

Ezra

3: 1-13   Verse 10 - Asaph was a Levite, the son of Barachias, and David's choir leader (see I Chron. 6:39). Those who wept were sad because the foundation of the temple did not appear as great as the first temple. They were looking in the natural instead of praising God they would have a temple to worship Him in.

(535 BC)

4: 4-5, 24   Adversaries showed up and the work on the House of the Lord ceased temporarily.

(Ezra continues after Haggai.)

****

(520 BC)
Haggai

1: 1-4, 8, 14	In the second year of the reign of Darius, God spoke through the prophet Haggai to Zerubbabel, governor of Judah, that the time had come to finish rebuilding the temple. They were building houses for themselves, but the House of the Lord still was not completed.
2: 1-9	God encouraged the people that He would be with them in the rebuilding; He also promised a time would come when the Glory of God would be seen even greater than in the original temple. (See **chapter 2: 7** & Mt. 21:9.)

The end of the book of Haggai

****

****

Ezra

(520 BC)

5: 1-5, 9-17	Work on the temple began again in 520 BC. Darius was now king. Sheshbazzar is the Babylonian name for Zerubbabel.

(515 BC)

6: 1-10, 15-22	The decree of Cyrus to rebuild the temple was found. *(This king Darius was not the same one that we read about in Daniel. See note after Daniel chapter 5.)* The chapter continues with the completion of the temple.

(457 BC)

7: 1, 6-23, 27-28	The son of Cyrus, referred to as Artaxerxes, was now king of Persia; he sent a letter of favor to Ezra. The copy of that commission begins in verse 11. Ezra had prepared his heart . . . Treasures were taken to beautify the House of the Lord.
8: 25, 31, 36	Chapter 8 is about Ezra's companions. Then, Ezra declared a fast. The offerings for the house of the Lord were taken to the king.
9: 1, 5-6, 15	The people of Israel were disobedient to the Lord. Ezra prayed.

(457 BC)

10: 1, 11   This is a continuation of chapter 9. It deals with Israel's plans to obey God, and separate themselves from the people of the surrounding lands. The chapter ends with a listing of those who had been disobedient.

The end of the book of Ezra

****

****

(521-509 BC)   *(The book of Esther has also been dated 485-474 BC which is the greatest dating discrepancy found in the noted study/reference books. Just remember that the exile to Babylon was over a period of time.)*

Esther

1: 2-12, 19, 22   King Ahasuerus of the Persian Empire held a feast.

(518 BC)

2: 1-11, 16-17, 21-22   The king sought for a new queen. Esther was prepared to go before the king to be chosen as a replacement for Queen Vashti. She didn't tell anyone she was a Jew. Esther was crowned Queen.

****

(510 BC)

3: 1-6, 8-14   Haman resented Queen Esther's uncle Mordecai for not bowing down before him. He found out Mordecai was a Jew and devised a plan to destroy the Jews.

4: 1-17   Esther prepared to appeal for Mordecai before the king.

5: 1-15   Esther appeared before the king.

6: 1-14   The king read in a book of records that a good deed was performed by Mordecai on behalf of the king and he had never been repaid.

****

7: 1-10   Esther admitted she was a Jew; Haman had planned the Jews destruction. The king had Haman put to death.

8: 1-17 (510 BC)	Feasting and gladness - The Jews avenged themselves.
9: 1-4, 17-22, 24, 26, 28-32	A feast was declared to celebrate the Jew's victory. They named this feast time Purim from the word pur which means cast lots to decide. Haman had cast lots in his decision to request the king to destroy the Jews.
(509 BC)	
10: 1- 3	Mordecai . . . (*Keep in mind that Almighty God was preserving the lineage for His Son Jesus, the coming Messiah, to be born.*)

The end of the book of Esther

****

****

(520-487 BC)

Zechariah

Some themes in Zechariah are as follows: People encouraged, Christ promised, Jerusalem to be restored.

Zechariah	
1: 1-4, 16-17	Darius was king of Assyria.
(519 BC)	
2: 10-11	
3: 8	Verses 1-7 tell Zechariah's vision; following the vision is a prophesy of the promised Messiah.
4: 5-6, 8-9	Zerubbabel was governor of Judah. This book is filled with Zechariah's prophetic visions seen by him in metaphorical symbols.
6: 12-13	Chapter 6 is another prophesy of the coming Messiah - the Kingdom of Christ.
(518 BC)	
7: 1, 4-14	The Lord rebuked His people; the conclusion is in chapter 8.

****

8: 1- 8, 11-23	Restoration promised. . .

(487 BC)

Zechariah

9: 9-10   Verses 1-8 are God speaking to the ungodly nations. Verse 9 is referring to the coming of Jesus (see Mt. 21:5).

****

10: 1-8, 12   Symbolic language is used to describe the corrupt shepherds/leaders. (Hiss means call them.)

11: 12-13   This is about Jesus - the cost of betrayal! (See Mt. 26:15 & 27:9.)

12: 1-2, **10**,   Chapters 12 & 13 continue to speak of future end times: rebellion, repentance, conversion, and blessing of the coming Messiah.

13: 1-3, **6-7**   In that day . . .

14: 3-5, 9   The second coming of Christ . . . In verse 5, the word flee means flee to safety. He is King of kings and Lord of Lords!

The end of the book of Zechariah

****

****

Nehemiah

(446- 445 BC)

(Nehemiah was born and raised in Babylon during the captivity; however, he was taught Hebrew ways and the Law. He sought God regarding the deplorable condition of Jerusalem and the Jews who had been left there. The city walls and gates had been destroyed by the Babylonians.

The captivity had ended; leave from Babylon had been granted to the Jews. Nehemiah, a cup bearer of King Artaxerxes in the Persian court, was commissioned by Artaxerxes to return to Jerusalem and rebuild the walls and gates of the city.)

1: 1-11   Nehemiah's prayer -

2: 1-20,   This was preparation to rebuild the wall, then opposition . . .

****

Nehemiah

	Chapter 3 lists the gates and who was assigned to repair them.
4: 1-23	Sanballat of Samaria and Tobiah the Ammonite mocked the workers. Nehemiah's prayer and his plan. . . The work continued.
5: 1-7,	There was a famine in Jerusalem, and some of the Jews were taking advantage of their poorer brothers. They were also required to sell
11-12,	their fields to pay the king's tax as well as other injustices and cruelty. Nehemiah was quite angry about what was happening to his brothers.
14-19	As governor, Nehemiah was allowed to require the people to supply his needs of "bread and wine" plus 40 shekels of silver for other expenses. He did not, but was kind to the poor and provided for his own needs.

****

6: 1-16	Sanballat's deceit - Nehemiah would not flee into the temple to save his life. The wall was finished in 52 days.
7: 1-5	Chapter 7 continues with genealogy being updated.
8: 1-18	The Feast of Tabernacles is one of the 3 feast that the Jewish people were commanded to celebrate each year. This one has not yet been fulfilled in the New Testament but the other two were.

****

Nehemiah 9	Take time to read this entire chapter even if it takes several days. They held a solemn feast, confessed sins, and acknowledged God's mercies.

****

10: 1, 38 -39	The Jews made a covenant with God and this chapter lists those who sealed it. Chapter 11 records distinct points of the covenant and
11: 1-2	continues regarding the dwellers of Jerusalem.
12: 27, 43- 45	Priests, Levites, and dedication of the wall . . . kept the ward meaning kept the charge or guard. . .
13: 1-12,	Nehemiah had been called back to Babylon by King Artaxerxes. During that time away the people disobeyed God's directions.
19-22,	Some men of Judah were bringing their products into the city to sell on

13: 29-31	the Sabbath. Nehemiah had the gates closed the evening before and on the Sabbath. He also gave commandment to the Levites regarding their wives.

End of the book of Nehemiah.
****

****

Malachi
(397 BC)

Malachi	*(Burden/load or thing lifted up; Esau/Edom - The Edomites were wicked people; God's treatment of Esau was hate compared to his love for Jacob.)*
1:1, 5-14	This is God's Word to Israel regarding their offering animals for sacrifice that were blind, lame, and/or sick instead of offering their best healthy animals. God is proclaiming *(those who are not Jews)* the Gentiles will come into God's kingdom.
2: 1-2, 4-11, 15- 17	The priests and the people were reproved; the men were divorcing their wives and marrying daughters of the heathens. God made male and female one (husband and wife) that He might have Godly offspring. *(Strange means stranger or foreigner; putting away is divorce; treacherously is defined as to deceive or depart.)*
3: 1-18	This is a prophesy that John the Baptist will come and tell about Jesus. *(Mt. 3: 11-12; Mt. 11:10 & 14)*. Then 7-12 speaks of God's blessings on those who will offer up their tithes. *(See II Corinthians 9: 6 -10 also.)*
4: 1-6	You shall be like calves released from the stall - leaping for joy. Verses **5-6** - Jesus stated in Mt. 11: 14 that John the Baptist was the Elijah (Elias) to come. *(The fathers are the Jews and the children are the Gentiles.)*

End of the book of Malachi
****

End of the Old Testament Survey
****

Appendix

Israelites Exit from Egypt (Goshen)

- Egypt (Goshen) east to
- Baalzephon; eastward across
- The Red Sea; south to
- Marah; continuing south to
- Elim; south to the
- Wilderness of Sin; and southeast toward
- Mt. Sinai (Horeb); north to
- Kadeshbarnea (edge of the Promised Land); to
- wandering in the wilderness for years before they could go back, and possess their promised lands.

They camped at Baalzephon by the Red Sea when they came out of Egypt. Then they camped at Elim (Manna distribution began there) on the way to the Wilderness of Sin on the way to Siani (Ex. 16). They arrived at Sinai the 15th. day of the 2nd. month after leaving Egypt.

Exodus 19 tells us it took less than 3 months to get to Horeb (Mt. Sinai) from Egypt. God gave the 10 Commandments and the Law there. *Note: Mt. Sinai is actually one mountain with 2 peaks. One is Mt. Sinai and the other Mt. Horeb.*

Telling of the journey from Sinai to Kadesh is in Numbers 10: 11 - 13 (In the 20th. day of the second month in the second year since coming out of Egypt). They traveled from the wilderness of Sinai through the wilderness of Paran on their way to Kadeshbarnea.

It is an eleven day journey from Horeb via Mt. Seir to Kadeshbarnea (the edge of the Promised Land). They were very close to the Promised Land when they camped at Kadesh (Deut. 1: 2, 19 - 20; 2: 46). This was Amorite country and they were supposed to possess it   but -

Deut. 1: 35, 40, 46 & 2: 1 tells us God instructed them to turn their direction from Kadeshbarnea into the wilderness because of their disobedience. (Around the mountain!)

so -

They wandered in the wilderness about 38 more years (40 in all since leaving Egypt) before they were allowed to enter the Promised Land, and then we find out what happened because they did not drive out all those inhabitants. Numbers 55:33 tells us what God said He would do if they didn't drive out all the inhabitants from their promised lands.

Maps Information

Maps of the Ancient Middle East can be found on the internet. The following maps would be helpful:

1. The Israelites exit from Egypt,
2. The location of the tribes after they received their inheritances,
3. A map of the Babylonian Empire,
4. Possibly one of the Medo Persian Empire.

The following is information that will assist in locating those maps:

- Bible history.com/maps/route exodus
- Ancient map of settlement of tribes
- Map of Ancient Near East

The following lists the twelve tribes of Israel and where they camped when the Tabernacle was raised up:

<u>East of the Tabernacle</u>
    Judah
    Issachar
    Zebulon

<u>On the south side</u>
    Reuben
    Simeon
    Gad

<u>Turning north on the west side</u>
    Ephraim
    Manasseh
    Benjamin

<u>Around toward the east on the north side would be</u>
    Dan
    Asher
    Naphtali

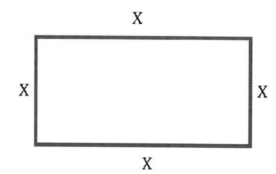

Closer to the Tabernacle (see the X's) camped Moses, Aaron, and the Levites: Moses, Aaron, and their families at the east gate; Kohath and family at the southern border; Gershon and family on the west; and the tribe of Merari on the north side.

The Tabernacle

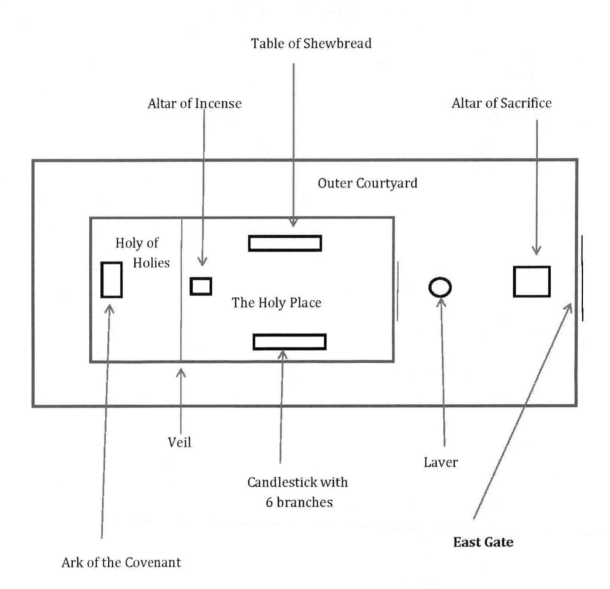

The measurements can be found in Exodus 25 and forward.

Kings of Israel: Saul, David, & Solomon, then the kingdom split.		
The following dates represent the time each king began to reign and are not exact. Some vary in different sources by as much as 30 years.		

(BC) **Kings of Israel**	*Prophets (BC dates)*	(BC) **Kings of Judah**
(975) Jeroboam		(975) Rehoboam
(954) Nadab		(958) Abijam/Abijah
(953) Baasha		(955) Asa
(930) Elah		(914) Jehoshaphat
(929) Zimri	*Elijah (910-896)*	
(929) Omri	↓	
(918) Ahab	*Elisha (896*	(892) Jehoram
(897) Ahaziah		(885) Ahaziah
(896) Jehoram (Joram)	*to*	(884) Athaliah, Queen
(884) Jehu		(878) Joash/Jehoash
(857) Jehoahaz	*838)*	(839) Amaziah
(839) Jehoash (Joash)		(810) Azariah /Uzziah
(825) Jeroboam	*Joel (800)*	
(773) Zechariah	*Amos (787)*	
(772) Shallum	*Hosea (785-725)*	(758) Jotham
(772) Menahem	*Isaiah (780-698)*	
(761) Pekahiah	*Micah (750-698)*	(742) Ahaz
(759) Pekah		
(730) Hoshea		
	Nahum (713)	(733) Hezekiah
(Fall of Samaria/Israel 721BC)		(704) Manasseh
	Zephaniah (680)	(649) Amon
		(641) Josiah
	Habakkuk (626)	(610) Jehoahaz
		(610) Jehoiakim/Eliakim
	Daniel (606-534)	(599) Jehoiachin/Jeconiah
		(599) Zedikiah/Mattaniah
	Ezekiel(595-575)	
	Obadiah (587)	*(After a 20 year siege, destruction of Jerusalem and exile completed - ~586 BC)*
	Jeremiah (581-586)	
	Ezra (536)	*Restoration began 538 BC (Ezra 1 & 2) (This was dated 536 in one of the sources utilized.) They returned to their own land as one nation - Israel.*
	Haggai (520-518)	
	Zechariah (520-518)	
		Rebuilding of Temple completed - (515 BC according to Ezra 6:15). Restoration continued until ~ 400 BC.)
	Nehemiah (446)	
	Malachi (397	

Isaiah 15 and 16 are one prophesy. The following descriptions/locations are listed in the order they appear:

- Ar of Moab was the capital city of Moab on the Arnon River, 17 miles east of the Dead Sea.
- Kir is an unknown location.
- Bajith & Dibon are high places; Dibon is on the eastern border of Moab north of the Arnon.
- Nebo was a place southwest of Heshbon overlooking the mouth of the Jordan River. This is also the name of a Babylonish god.
- Medeba is south of Heshbon.
- Baldness was a heathen custom of mourning for the dead. To lose a beard (cut off beard) was also a sign of mourning. A full long beard was a highly coveted ornament. See Lev. 21: 15.
- Heshbon was east of the Jordan River on the boundary between the territories of Reuben and Gad.
- Elealeh was east of Jordan in Moab, north of Heshbon.
- Jahaz not identified as yet.
- Zoar was on the east side of the Dead Sea, northeast of Jordan.
- Luhith was a pass somewhere in Moab not yet identified.
- Horonaim is a cavern near Zoar.
- Brook of the Willows was a valley of the Arabians.
- Beerelim refers to a well of heroes.
- Dimon refers to streams east of the Dead Sea in Moab.

Chapter 16
- Sela/Selah/Petra is an Edomite city; Petra is the Greek translation of Sela. This was a stronghold in Edom, the country settled by Esau's descendants who were always idolaters.
- Daughter of Zion is Jerusalem.
- Daughters of Moab - Daughters refers to those who hold the faith of that place. It also could be suburbs or villages of that place mentioned.
- Fords of Arnon (river) - Fords are places of crossing a river by wading.

- Kirhareseth/Kirharesh was one of the chief fortified cities of Moab that was 10 miles from the Dead Sea.
- Heshbon was the capital city of Sihon king of the Amorites on the western border of the Mishor.
- Sibmah was east of Jordan in the tribe of Reuben's area.
- Jazer/Jaazer was an Amorite town east of Jordan, west of Ammon, and north of Heshbon which was famous for its vineyards.
- Elealeh was east of Jordan on the plateau of Moab, northeast of Heshbon.

More of God's Purposes
for the Written Word:

"For whatsoever things were written aforetime were written for our learning, that we through patience and comfort of the scriptures might have hope." (Romans 15: 4, KJV)

1. To know God created the universe; only He is almighty, all knowing, and eternal. He is all righteous, just, and merciful. God is love; the sins that continued to provoke His wrath in the Old Covenant were pride and idol worship.
2. God spoke the events that were to come to pass, through prophets, so that no one could credit their false deities as having performed the miracles done by Almighty God. Then He had the information written for us to see and learn.
3. Details of the sinful nature of humanity, repentance, and God's restoration in the lives of our ancestors were provided for our learning. We can see, due to Adam's disobedience and submission to the devil's plan, that unregenerate man quickly submits to evil instead of trusting our unseen God. The scriptures also provide details of those who trusted God and kept believing in Him even when they sinned and circumstances became wearisome. We are to see their mistakes, and learn from them. (See I Corinthians 10: 1-14.)
4. Almighty God provided a Savior - The genealogy of Jesus the Messiah can be traced throughout the Old Testament. God used His prophets to speak the future into being.
5. Jesus is coming back and those who believed God under the old covenant and those who trusted Jesus for their salvation under the new covenant, will spend eternity with our Glorious God. (Those living in the Old Testament times did not understand that there would be two comings of the Messiah.)

****

*The Lord bless you and keep you: The Lord make His face
shine upon you, and be gracious unto you: The Lord lift
up His countenance upon you, and give you peace.
(Numbers 6: 24-26, KJV)*

Printed in the United States
By Bookmasters